The
Shackling
of
Grace

How The Church Has

Marginalized

The Grace of God

Lee LeFebre

All scripture references are from the
New King James and King James Versions
unless otherwise marked

Available at:
www.leelefebre.com
www.thelifebookstore.com
www.amazon.com

With no hestitation, I dedicate this book to my
beautiful, faithful, loving bride who has
laid her life down for me for over 50 years.
She enables me to fulfill my passionate call
to teach the unshackled grace of God.
She facilitates and encourages our sons
to lead their families and be
successful fathers, husbands and models
for our 15 grandchildren.
Without her stability, love,
and organizational skills,
I would still be typing term papers!

Contents

Part 3 — Results

Introduction

As you read through this book, you will know that I have spent my life teaching people how God intends to have us know and experience the finished work of Christ in such a way that it transforms our thinking, feeling, choices, behavior, and speech. Yes, our entire life can be transformed.

As a teacher I would like to make sure that you learn the essentials of what is called, "The Exchanged Life"—or in this case the obstacles, which I call *The Shackling of Grace.* My prayer is that this book will transform your life in a tangible way.

I encourage you to flip to Appendix A and take the Kwiki Kwiz now, before you read this book. It will serve as a reference point for your beliefs. After you have read the book, take

Kwiki Kwiz #2 in Appendix B. I think you will find it enlightening to compare your answers.

If you are uncertain of the correct answers, go to our website—www.elmco.org/ and click on "Grace Encounters."

Finally, as you read through this text you will note that many verses, or passages of Scripture, are oft-repeated. This was necessary to properly convey the full meaning behind the message and how it is to be applied experientially.

Part 1

False Beliefs

Chapter One

Becoming a Better Sinner

God creates out of nothing.
Wonderful you say. Yes, to be sure,
but he does what is still more wonderful:
he makes saints out of sinners.
Soren Kierkegaard

"Becoming a Better Sinner": I have seldom come across a title which is both honest and descriptive of so many Christians. It is fair to say teaching me to "become a better sinner" was the primary objective of nearly every church I attended from youth to adulthood.

I owe the chapter title to a man of the cloth who wrote an article addressing the issue a few years ago. In reading the article I was shocked at what an incredible lack of Biblical understanding the writer displayed on the very topic he was addressing. Yet I also realized that the vast majority of evangelical churches would agree with his view.

I decided the Reverend's title could be put into a question. Simply stated, "Are you trying to become a better sinner?"

To ask this question is like asking a thief, "Are you trying to become a better thief?" This question could be applied to liars, rapists, sexual offenders, and numerous other well-labeled sinners. Interestingly, I would suggest the majority of church members today would answer "No!" to these questions, but "Yes!" in response to becoming a better sinner. Is this question suggesting you are trying to become a more skillful sinner or trying to sin less and less?

An Inadequate View

To better lay the groundwork for this point of view let me quote directly from one of the two magazine articles that, although very similar in wording, were written about four years apart—indicating the writer's commitment to his words and his view.

> "Simply put, we are not capable of not sinning.... David's adultery with Bathsheba and murder of Uriah certainly qualifies him as a sinner; yet God describes him as 'a man after God's own heart.' ....if David was a man after God's own heart, does that mean he was also somehow

a sinner after God's own heart? If so . . . what would that look like? ....The Bible separates our salvation into two important functions. *Justification* — the settling of our accounts regarding sin.

The other dynamic in redemption is called *sanctification*. This refers to the ongoing, difficult process of Christ being 'formed in us.' Sanctification involves a process of growth, one that continues through every day of our lives until eventually we reach the Day promised in Revelation 21 when Jesus will 'make all things new' and will 'wipe away every tear from our eyes.' ....God justifies us when we, by faith, receive the salvation he offers through Christ. ....But God's process of making us new usually takes longer than that. Much longer. [We are] still sinners. Always sinners this side of that loud trumpet blast, but steadily becoming much healthier sinners. ....In short, *better* sinners. ....Maybe our trouble isn't on the *outside* but rather on the *inside.* That's what the prophet Jeremiah seems to point to with his dark diagnosis: 'The heart is deceitful above all things and beyond cure (Jeremiah 17:9). ....We not only *commit* sins, we are sinful. It's part of us.''*

* Rev. Ron Vanderwell, *The Banner,* a publication of the Christian Reformed Church — 2007 and 2011

I do not know the writer, except through this article. He just happens to be the person who is honest about the objective of thousands of teachers and pastors who, whether they know it or not, are teaching their flocks to become better sinners. As a pastor who was taught the total depravity of all humanity, he believes that depravity still leaks from Christian adults.

"There is a myth passed along among Christians that we can conquer sin in our lives. It's hinted at in our conversations, reinforced in songs we listen to, and sometimes preached with vigor from our pulpits. Given enough time, enough willpower, enough of the right conferences or radio programs or religious paperbacks, we should be able to get our spiritual acts fully together.

The Bible seems to support this point of view. The book of Romans speaks freely about being ....*dead to sin* (6:2). Even Jesus himself calls us to ....*be perfect, therefore as your heavenly Father is perfect* (Matthew 5:48)."

On the contrary however, be assured, neither the Bible, nor I, assert that Christians can conquer sin. What the Bible says is that Christ conquered sin by dying to sin. Note how clear Romans 6:10 states the method that Christ used to conquer sin... *For the death that He died, He died to sin once for all; but the life that He lives, He lives to God.*

How does that help us? When Christ died to sin, we were in Christ and died to sin with him. Romans 6:11 reads... *Likewise you also, reckon yourselves to be dead indeed to sin, but alive to God in Christ Jesus our Lord.* Romans 6:17 further states.... *But God be thanked that though you were slaves to sin, yet you obeyed from the heart that form of doctrine to which you were delivered.* Note, these verses do not say that sin or temptation died!

Why do so many Christians doubt that Christ's victory is our victory over sin? First, I believe that they do not know what "in Christ" means. Second, they do not distinguish between the power of sin in Romans 6, and the behavior called sin mentioned, for example, in 1 John 1. Third, they look at their track record in responding to temptation instead of the finished work of Christ detailed in Scripture. Fourth, they can point to 1 Timothy 1:15 where Paul exclaims that "I (Paul) am the chief of sinners.

Paul's statement needs a closer look because it is in the present tense making this verse perhaps the best argument that we are still sinners. More is expounded on this subject in chapter seven—*Identity Theft.*

As Christian author, Bill May, writes in Volume 15, Number 7 of his newsletter called *The Christian....* "When Christ is our life and center, his relationship with all things becomes ours.... Apart from Christ we do not have a proper relationship with anything." He goes on to say, "On the positive side, Christ is our relationship with the Father. He is also our relationship with all the saints, the members of his body. On the negative side, Christ is our relationship with sin.... the flesh, the world, condemnation, the devil, and the law."

When Vanderwell looks at his track record, as well as the history of other Christians, he writes the following....

> "It would seem we're supposed to get past this sin problem. But somehow we never quite outgrow our taste for iniquity. Over time we learn to curb some of our behaviors, and some temptations genuinely subside as the Holy Spirit settles deeper into our hearts. But our bias toward evil never seems to completely vanish, no matter how hard we try to leave it behind. We still lose our temper, even if the words we say sound a little more acceptable. We still harbor grudges, even if our resentments now center on more noble causes. We still turn to lust to provide secret comforts or obsess over food or "toys" to soothe our stress. We still strain to buy the best technology or the most impressive clothing we can, even if it loads our credit cards with debt. We still scurry around in the clouds of self-importance, neglecting the needs of those closest to us. And even on the days we do manage to resist such temptations, a candid look might

show us how much our apparent holiness is actually prompted by lesser motives: avoiding guilt or having to explain things to an accountability partner."

This begs the question, "Is this what you believe? Does this resonate with your experience? Do you believe, as the writer does that, we are not capable of *not* sinning?

The writer also runs to Romans 7, as do thousands of other Christians, to find comfort in Paul's wretched cry, *...for what I am doing, I do not understand. For what I will to do, that I do not practice; but what I hate, that I do* (Romans 7:15). When the writer turns to David's sin with Bathsheba, he tries to comfort his readers with the passage where God describes David as "a man after God's own heart."

There now.... when you read Romans 7 and God's comment about David after his sins of adultery and murder, don't you feel better? This kind of comfort is fed to Christians day-after-day, week-after-week, month-after-month, and year-after-year, both in person and from the pulpit.

What is Really at Stake?

The most fundamental mistake I find throughout the church today is the idea that identity and behavior are inseparable. The church teaches us we can never break free from the "such a worm as I" mentality, because, as the Reverend points out, "We are not capable of not sinning....because we continue to leak total depravity." In other words, this part of the good news is only applicable to the next life, and sanctification is limited to a process of gradually being cleaned up to the status of being a "better sinner."

What is at stake here is the totality and completeness of what God did on our behalf, through the death and resurrection of his son.

Am I suggesting that we, as Christians, no longer sin? Absolutely not! However, I am saying that in spite of our occasional wrong behavior, our identity has been permanently changed, reflecting a life that is eternal in nature and being.

Most teaching limits sanctification to a present/ future process, and leaves a believer stuck with a lowly identity riddled with shame and guilt. If sanctification is confined to the future, how do Christians reconcile scriptures like, "you are complete in Christ.... a holy people.... the righteousness of God in Christ.... perfected for all time.... a new creation"

The word sanctification means "holiness, to set apart." To sanctify, therefore, means "to make holy." To sanctify someone or something is to set that person or thing apart for the use intended by its designer.

The past tense of sanctify is used at least fifteen times in the New Testament. It is spoken of, not as a process, but as a completed act of the Lord Jesus when God placed us in Christ, executed us with the Lord Jesus, buried us, raised us and enthroned us. *If (since) then you were raised with Christ, seek those things which are above, where Christ is, sitting at the right hand of God. Set your mind on things above, not on things on the earth. For you died, and your life is hidden with Christ in God* (Colossians 3:1-3). Note the tense of these verses.

Sanctification in the Old Testament

One of my theological consultants, Dr. David Orison, president of *Grace for the Heart,* wrote the following:

> First, it is God who sanctifies and he does so by association. Israel was sanctified because she was set apart to be his. The vessels of the tabernacle and temple were sanctified because they were set apart for worship of him. The priests were sanctified because they served him. The sabbath was sanctified because it was set apart by and for the Lord. Several times in the Scriptures we read, "For I am the Lord who sanctifies you." That means they were holy/sanctified because he was holy/sanctified and they belonged to him.
>
> Another thing seen in the Old Testament is that the people were often called to sanctify them-

selves. Before they crossed the dry Jordan River, Joshua called the people to sanctify themselves. Before they identified Achan as the one who stole the booty and hid it in his house, Joshua told the people to sanctify themselves. The bearers of the Ark were to sanctify themselves before their holy work. There was a distinction between their normal daily life and their appearance before the Lord. Anytime the people entered the presence of the Lord or did special work of worship, they were to sanctify themselves.

Now, I don't see this anywhere in the New Testament. I do not believe this is a New Covenant concept, although I suspect it lies behind such things as dressing up in our 'Sunday best' and giving things up for Lent. I also suspect that many preachers and teachers have this in mind when they talk about sanctification as a process.

Point two: The idea that we can do something to sanctify ourselves or make ourselves holy is not a New Covenant concept. While the New Covenant between God and the people was different because of Jesus, we have no particular reason to think that the process of sanctification was different. We are still sanctified by association. Sanctification is not something separate from the person of Jesus Christ. He is our sanctification, according to Paul. *But of Him you are in*

Christ Jesus, who became for us wisdom from God—and righteousness and sanctification and redemption (1 Corinthians 1:30).

His life has sanctified us. We are holy because he is holy, just like he said. He is holy and we are holy because he is in us and we are in him. Our identity in Christ was given to us, once and forever, as a gift—nothing of our work or character or sacrifice was in it. And with that identity came sanctification, once and forever. *By that will we have been sanctified through the offering of the body of Jesus Christ once for all* (Hebrews 10:10).

Because we are associated with Jesus, and I mean that in the strongest terms, we are sanctified. We live in relationship with him. We are more intimately connected to him than we could be with any other person. He lives in us and we live in him. This association is our identity.

I know there are some who will say that we can lose that relationship because of wrong actions or attitudes. I don't believe that. I did nothing to get this relationship except to receive it and I do nothing to maintain the relationship. I believe that I will belong to Jesus for eternity because he is my life. There is no me apart from him.

Point three: My sanctification/holiness comes to me only and always through Jesus. He is the holy one and he makes me holy just by association. So now the question remains as to whether there is some kind of process of sanctification. How could that be true if sanctification is simply a fact of our relationship with Jesus? What kind of process would make sense? Would I become more holy? Would I somehow keep myself holy? Do we somehow redefine sanctification when it comes to living out the Christian life? Are there two definitions allowed by scripture?

Well the problem with proof-texting is that we start from an assumption and look to the scriptures to affirm it. If we start with the idea that sanctification is a process, something like what the people did for themselves in the Old Covenant, then we will probably find it in the New Testament scriptures. But we don't have to do that.

Let's look at a couple of passages. *For both He who sanctifies and those who are being sanctified are all of one, for which reason He is not ashamed to call them brethren* (Hebrews 2:11). *For by one offering He has perfected forever those who are being sanctified* (Hebrews 10:14).

Much is made of this idea of "being sanctified." However, the word "being" is not in the text. It is an inflection of the word "sanctified" that allows a continuous action. The KJV and the

NASB both chose "are sanctified." But if we remember that this action is accomplished only by the Lord and only through our association with him, we find the answer.

The connection between us and the Lord is a continual process. Not a process of becoming, but a process of being. We have no holiness apart from him. Holiness is in us because he is in us. But our connection with him is dynamic. We live in a real and active relationship with him. He is continually holy in us and we are continually holy in him. We don't become more holy, but we are continually being made holy (sanctified) in him. It isn't that we can lose this, but simply that he is continually active within us.

Point Four: Our sanctification is a done deal, a finished work, once and forever—because it is in Jesus. But his life in us is dynamic, living and active. It is always responsible to note verses that seem out of sync with a teaching. For example, *Now may the God of peace Himself sanctify you completely; and may your whole spirit, soul, and body be preserved blameless at the coming of our Lord Jesus Christ* (1 Thessalonians 5:23).

In what way has God not sanctified us completely? It is difficult to harmonize this verse with any idea of sanctification. I suspect that it is simply a blessing in which Paul reminds his readers at the end of his letter that God is at work in them and has claimed them as his own. He makes it very clear, in the next verse, that sanctification is the sole work of God. *Pursue peace with all people* , and holiness, without which no one will see the Lord (Hebrews 12:14).

Finally we come to the process of spiritual growth, as Major Ian Thomas said, "becoming who we are." Any idea of pursuing holiness (same word as sanctification) can only mean the transforming of our thinking to conform with the mind of Christ, which is already active and resident within us. We are certainly a becoming people, as far as outward behavior is concerned. The day will come when our behavior will fully and forever become consistent with who we are.

But is this sanctification? It seems both incorrect and unhelpful to say that it is. This is spiritual growth, the "working out of our salvation." We do not become more saved or more sanctified through this process. We simply draw a little closer in our understanding to the identity that is ours in Christ."

Sanctification involves a renewal of the mind. Are we saved by grace and sanctified by works? If along with the Reverend we quoted earlier in the chapter we buy into the belief of sanctification by our works, then sanctification for all of us will be an "ongoing and difficult process." We will be attempting to duplicate needlessly the finished work of Christ. This duplication will be impossible and is what makes Christians burn out and too often drop out.

Before the Cross

The unbelieving Jew and Gentile and even the believing Jew in the Old Testament (Old Covenant) were at a tremendous disadvantage compared to the New Covenant believer. In Ephesians 2:12 Paul said to Christians, *....at that time you were without Christ, being aliens from the commonwealth of Israel and strangers from the covenants of promise, having no hope and without God in the world.* He was referring to their pre-Christian days.

The Old Covenant Jews did not have God indwelling as we do. When the judges, kings, and prophets spoke on behalf of God, the Spirit would come upon them and then depart. Of course the law, which was their primary restraint, was locked up in the tabernacle. Is it any wonder God says to the people of Judah, *The heart is deceitful above all things, and desperately wicked, who can know it?* (Jeremiah 17:9). Is this then the believer's condition in the New Covenant?

David, after his sin with Bathsheba, pleaded in Psalm 51:10 for a clean heart and a steadfast spirit. Through Ezekiel God prophesied that he would fulfill David's request by cleansing his people from sin. God also promised, *....I will give you a new heart and put a new spirit within you; I will take the heart of stone out of your flesh and give you a heart of flesh. I will put My Spirit within you and cause you to walk in My statutes, and you will keep My judgments and do them* (Ezekiel 36:26-27). When did this occur? It was accomplished and available for the first time after Pentecost!

In addition, Romans 7 talks of the Jew who lived under law (count the number of times that law is mentioned in this chapter), and Paul says that when we were in the flesh (not in Christ), *....sinful passions which were aroused by the law were at work in our members to bear fruit to death* (Romans 7:5). Does this sound like a man who has died to the law? Paul continues to make the distinction between past and present, *But now we have been delivered from the law, having died to what we were held by* (Romans 7:6).

A thorough understanding of these truths is vital for discovering the fulness of the victorious life that God has so graciously and freely provided for his beloved children.

Is It Time For a New Reformation?

After reading through the Reverend's complete articles, I was left with the thought, "If this is all the Bible offers, we are in serious trouble." But more likely it is time that the Bible is studied for purposes of another

Reformation. If the writer is correct, then God is suspect when he says through Paul, *How shall we who died to sin live any longer in it?* (Romans 6:2).

Most Christians will, of course, give credit to God for any progress gained in their fight against sin, referenced as sanctification. You may have noticed, as I have, that many believers get more crotchety as they get older. What does this tell you about their success in becoming sanctified by works?

The Ultimate Decision

Do you fully realize that salvation is by grace alone—a free gift? Do you realize that sanctification as taught in the New Covenant is also a free gift?

Vanderwell apparently believes it is helpful to think of sinners much like the world sees addicts. That is, we will always be recovering sinners, as we gradually become better sinners.

God tells us we are new creations, saints, the elect, pure, holy, righteous, without blemish. *He chose us in Him before the foundation of the world, that we should be holy and without blame before Him in love, ...to the praise of the glory of His grace, by which He made us accepted in the Beloved* (Ephesians 1:4,6). And... *if anyone is in Christ, he is a new creation; old things have passed away; behold, all things have become new, ...For He made Him who knew no sin to be sin for us, that we might become the righteousness of God in Him* (2 Corinthians 5:17, 21).

As Charles Trumbull said in his book, *Victory in Christ,* "It is not that we are not able to sin, but it is that we are able not to sin."

Do you, Reverend, believe we are a new creation? Or are we just an old creation, cleansed and forgiven through numerous confessions and continuous forgiveness?

Romans 5:8 reads, *But God demonstrates His own love toward us, in that while we were still(yet) sinners, Christ died for us.* The clear implication of this verse is that Christ's death took place when we were sinners, but we are sinners no longer. What do those who believe we are still sinners do with this verse? Ignore it? Paul too believes that what was true about us, before Christ died for us, is no longer true! Yet many people believe we are still sinners because of passages like 1 Timothy 1:15, ... *that Christ Jesus came into the world to save sinners, of whom I am chief.*

As we look closely at that passage and put it into context, I believe we see a powerful argument in Paul's own statement that would refute that view. In verse 13 of that passage Paul states, *....although I was formerly a blasphemer, a persecutor, and an insolent man; but I obtained mercy because I did it ignorantly in unbelief.*

In the book of Acts however, in Paul's appeal to Caesar, he says, *"I stand at Caesar's judgment seat, where I ought to be judged. To the Jews I have done no wrong, as you very well know. For if I am an offender, or have committed anything deserving of death, I do not object to dying; but if there is nothing in these things of which these men accuse me, no one can deliver me to them. I appeal to Caesar."*

On the one hand Paul says that God had mercy earlier in his life because he acted in ignorance. But now, he knows the truth, and the truth is he is no longer that man who was a sinner in the eyes of God, but is now free from that identity and curse.

Assume for a moment that you were the champion pole vaulter in your high school. As you take someone on a tour of the gym they see your many trophies. If they ask, "Who is the champion of all pole vaulters in your school," you could answer "I am!" Present tense. Does that mean you are still pole vaulting? No it doesn't because you are now 72 years old and would break your silly neck.

So it was with Paul. He could say in the present tense, "I am chief of sinners," because he held the record, not because he was still a sinner.

Who is telling the truth—God or man? We must not be tempted to ignore the truth of the Word of God.

Chapter Two

Making a Mockery
of Faith

Faith is taking the first step
even when you don't see
the whole staircase.
Martin Luther King, Jr.

How can we make a mockery of faith? Do you know that it is possible to shackle grace by utilizing false concepts of living by faith? It is relatively common to say that our denomination is our faith, or that Christianity is our faith. It is also common to affirm that we have faith that we will be healed, or that we will become prosperous if we send tithe money to the wealthy pastors begging on television. Have you noticed the "name it and claim it" tithe proponents make sure you send the tithe to their personal ministries?

Do we hear about what it means that we, as children of the light, are enjoined to walk by faith rather than by sight. When we walk by sight we can live as the unbeliever lives, by putting our faith solely in the functions of the soul and body.

A person who lives by sight trusts in the three parts of the soul which are pictured here:

SOUL OR PERSONALITY

Will — Choose

Mind — Think

Emotions — Feel

In addition, the person who lives by sight places his confidence in the functions of the body as pictured here:

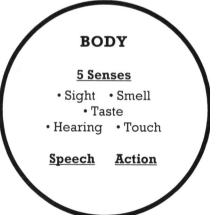

BODY

5 Senses

• Sight   • Smell
• Taste
• Hearing   • Touch

Speech   **Action**

Thus a person who functions out of the body and soul can read the Bible, pray, fast, practice yoga, and even produce facsimiles of the fruit of the Spirit. However if one of the essential components of a person is dead to God, absent or not utilized, it is impossible to live by spiritual faith.

Each of us is born with a human spirit which is intangible and invisible like the soul. But the spirit is separate from the soul. Since it is invisible, people may not even know that they have a human spirit.

The human spirit was intended, from creation, to be a vessel or container of the Holy Spirit, which is a person of the Godhead. Without an awareness of the spirit, and especially without the indwelling Spirit of God, it is impossible to live by spiritual faith. However, it is granted that an incomplete person can live by psychological faith, which is useless for faith in God. Thus the Bible describes such a person as "in Adam" and without God. *At that time you were without Christ, being aliens from the commonwealth of Israel and strangers from the covenants of promise, having no hope and without God in the world* (Ephesians 2:12).

I encourage you to study the graphic on the following page.

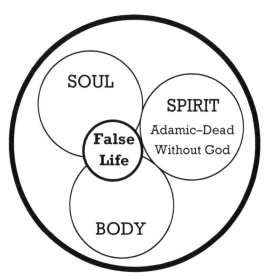

Major Ian Thomas describes a person without Christ as being like a lamp without oil or a car without gas.

Since Christ said he was the Life, a person who tries to live the Christian life out of a 2-part being (soul and body) is living an imitation of Christ's life. It may look like Christ's life, but Christ's life cannot be imitated. Therefore it is a false life.

Living by the Spirit

God intended for us to live by faith in the invisible realm. He intended for us to live by what we cannot see. But how do we do that? Hebrews 11:1 tells us that....*faith is the substance of things hoped for, the evidence of things not seen.*

God intended for the New Covenant believer to

live by the Spirit and by his position in Christ in the heavenlies, even while living in the visible world with a physical body. Man is the only created being that can live by sight and/or by faith. The soul can live exclusively by the functions of itself or the body and the soul can live by the Spirit, which is the invisible realm which includes the reality of our position in Christ. 2 Corinthians 4:18 reads, *....we do not look at the things which are seen, but at the things which are not seen. For the things which are seen are temporary, but the things which are not seen are eternal.*

How did it happen that Christians adopted a dichotomous (two part) view of man? It happened in much the same way that a false view of a Singer sewing machine would be gained by reading a Ford truck manual.

The wrong manuals (secular psychology) are read to determine how God created man. Man wrote his own manuals and believed them rather than the Bible.

In Genesis we read that, *The Lord God formed man of the dust of the ground* (body), *and breathed into his nostrils the breath of life* (spirit), *and man became a living being* (soul), (Genesis 2:7). God said man was very good, but he did not say man was perfect or complete. He had not eaten of the tree of life which would have joined him to God, because the tree of life was eternal life, or God's life. Thus the tree of life would have made man complete.

Not only in Genesis do we read that man is a three-part creature (trichotomist), but also in 1 Thessalonians 5:23, *Now may the God of peace Himself sanctify you completely; and may your whole spirit, soul, and body be preserved blameless at the coming of our Lord Jesus Christ.*

The Wrong Manual Continued

Why then do so many Christians, perhaps the vast majority of the evangelical church, teach man is a two-part being?

My friend, author and movie producer, Greg Smith as well as Gene Edwards, well known Christian author, believe it happened as follows. Quoting Smith:

> "The early Greek philosophers speculated that man had two parts, body and soul, the material and the immaterial. Socrates cemented that thought into his philosophy, as did Plato, his pupil, and Aristotle, Plato's pupil. The philosophies of these three men, who lived centuries before Jesus' birth, have formed the basis of Western thought for 2500 years.
>
> All three men taught, 'Man is body and soul.' Their writings, until this very day, are held as almost sacred throughout the earth. Their influence on our lives is nothing less than staggering.... It has been said, 'A person born in the

West cannot think unless he thinks Aristotle.' "

Other men of influence still have impact upon today's Christian leaders including Origen, a Hebrew who incorporated much Greek philosophical thinking into his teaching. Augustine (A.D. 354-430) who, as an early church father, taught that man was only body and soul. The teachings of these men became part of early church tradition. Even after the Reformation traditions survived and outweighed the Scriptures in many instances. Augustine also elevated the intellect as the primary way to know God. Catholics, and some Protestants, gave supernatural credibility to Augustine's teaching at the expense of Scripture. Further influence in church teaching came from Thomas Aquinas.

Finally, 500 years later, Jesse Penn-Lewis, Mary McDonough, T. Austin Sparks, and my personal hero, Watchman Nee, all challenged the two-part view of man and moved significant numbers in the church toward a three-part view of man. But how often do we hear the names of these people in teaching and preaching?

What Difference Does It Make?

Jesus needed a dwelling place in his new temple—his vessel called man. He needed a Holy of Holies! The body wouldn't do, because it was in the process of decay. The soul, also known as the personality, wasn't a proper place for Christ. It was forever changing and was often a vehicle for evil. The spirit, which died to God and became alive to God's enemy in the Genesis fall also fell short of God's holiness. However, what if the human spirit could be replaced? Replace it is what God did as prophesied by Ezekiel in Chapter 36:26-27, *I will give you a new heart and put a new spirit within you; I will take the heart of stone out of your flesh and give you a heart of flesh. I will put My Spirit within you ....*

Now, Christ has a dwelling place. Now, there is room in the Inn. Therefore the New Covenant reads, *But he who is joined to the Lord is one spirit with Him* (1 Corinthians 6:17). This is now the basis for becoming a new creation. God is no longer outside his temple, or symbolically confined to the Holy of Holies. The curtain to the Holy of Holies was rent in twain at the crucifixion in order that the Spirit of God could move from the Holy of Holies (in a building made with human hands) and move into a temple now made without human hands—you and me at the new birth. What is the difference? *the Most High does not dwell in temples made with hands, as the prophet says: 'Heaven is My throne, And earth is My footstool. What house will you build for Me? says the Lord, Or what is the place of My rest?*(Acts 7:48-49). His temple is the Christian believer!

Chapter Three

The Galatian Error

I can say, Christ has been
my only object; thank God,
my righteousness too...
Hold fast to Christ.
John Nelson Darby

In his letter to the Galatian church, Paul addressed a problem—a problem that had much to do with his fellow missionary, Simon Peter. In Paul's letter to the Galatians he said he confronted Peter in Antioch. *Now when Peter had come to Antioch, I withstood him to his face, because he was to be blamed* (Galatians 2:11). What was Peter's offense? Jewish law forbade eating with the uncircumcised Gentiles, but Peter regularly ate with the Gentile Christians—except when other Jews were around. When the Jews came around, Peter and Barnabas displayed double-mindedness, by not dining with the gentiles.

In our society, most Christians would be quite comfortable breaking bread with a Jew. However, it was of major consequence in Galatia and even though the circumstances differ today, the hypocrisy remains.

As the passage continues Paul addresses the fact that we are justified by faith and not by works of the law. He calls trying to be justified by law a matter of rebuilding those things which he destroyed which would make him a lawbreaker. *For if I build again those things which I destroyed, I make myself a transgressor* (Galatians 2:18).

This problem was bigger than we think. Imagine yourself a Gentile in that day. Paul taught in his letter to the Ephesians, *Therefore remember that you, once Gentiles in the flesh—who are called Uncircumcision by what is called the Circumcision made in the flesh by hands—that at that time you were without Christ, being aliens from the commonwealth of Israel and strangers from the covenants of promise, having no hope and without God in the world. But now in Christ Jesus you who once were far off have been brought near by the blood of Christ. For He Himself is our peace, who has made both one, and has broken down the middle wall of separation, having abolished in His flesh the enmity, that is, the law of commandments contained in ordinances, so as to create in Himself ONE new man from the two, thus making peace, and that He might reconcile them both to God in one body through the cross, thereby putting to death the enmity* (Ephesians 2:11-16). In spite of Paul's teaching, church leaders were practicing and teaching adherence to the law and separation from Gentiles.

A Simplistic View

We would be too simplistic if we merely took these Scriptures to mean that we as Christians, must accept Gentiles and Christian Jews as equals and treat them as such. Certainly it means that, but there is so much more. Paul was by no means through with his discussion on the topic.

The Jewish converts had a long-held view that they were better than other people and races in the world. They scornfully referred to the Gentiles as "the uncircumcised" in their conversations. Assuredly, the Gentiles were aware of this attitude of superiority on the part of the Jews. When the Gentiles became Christians, they thought the Jewish attitudes would change, but they didn't. The Jews were talking the talk but not walking it out in practice. Therefore, Paul refers to them as hypocrites.

The Jews saw themselves as superior to others for one reason or another. Today, some Christians might see themselves as better worshipers, speakers, mothers or friends than other Christians. All these examples, however, have one thing in common. They are based on self-righteousness, which in reality, is no righteousness at all.

Galatians 2:20

Sometimes I fear Christians misuse this cherished verse. We use it to prove that we were crucified with Christ, and now, ...*not I, but Christ lives in me*. This is true, but the context is that Paul is dealing with the Galatian error of self-righteousness.

How is self-righteousness accrued? It is accrued by meeting people's expectations by living a more acceptable lifestyle, and by conforming to the norms of our society, our church, our home and our friends. When we ask ourselves whether or not we are good Christians, the common response is to look at performance—thoughts, choices, emotions, behavior, actions, and speech—and decide whether or not they qualify us as "good." We, in effect, judge ourselves by whether we have measured up to our internal and external standards—our law system. After all, that is what we have been taught to work on all our lives.

To this kind of system, which we use to judge ourselves and others, Paul says, *I do not set aside the grace of God; for if righteousness comes through the law* (behavior)*, then Christ died in vain* (Galatians 2:21).

Foolish Galatians

O foolish Galatians! Who has bewitched you that you should not obey the truth, before whose eyes Jesus Christ was clearly portrayed among you as crucified? (Galatians 3:1). Paul might as well have said, "Where are you getting your information? Have you gone to see a witch?"

This only I want to learn from you: Did you receive the Spirit by the works of the law, or by the hearing of faith? (Galatians 3:2). In other words, "How did you become a Christian? Did you have to work at it? Cleaning up your thinking, choices, emotions, speech, behavior and action? Or did you accept the free gift of Christ Jesus Himself?"

Are you so foolish? Having begun in the Spirit, are you now being made perfect by the flesh? Have you suffered so many things in vain—if indeed it was in vain? (Galatians 3:3-4). This is asking the Galatians, "Once you become a Christian, do you think that you can become a better Christian by being circumcised or by not eating with the uncircumcised?"

In our day and age, do we believe we can become better Christians, or even superior Christians, by reading our Bible more, praying more, witnessing more and cleaning up our thought life? Could we get closer to God by thinking of Him more or attending church more often? To all this, Paul asks, "Who taught you these things? A witch? Where are you getting your information? Don't be foolish. If you think you are saved by faith and made perfect by works, your thinking is wrong. You're deceived!"

Only By Faith

Paul's point to the Galatians was not about having more faith in God in order to become better Christians. He was challenging them to accept, by faith, something God wanted them to trust in and rely on—something that is true about us in the invisible part of us—our spirit.

When we received Christ, God deposited himself in our spirit as his gift of righteousness. *For if by the one man's offense death reigned through the one, much more those who receive abundance of grace and of the gift of righteousness will reign in life through the One, Jesus Christ* (See Romans 5:17). *....and be found in Him, not having my own righteousness, which is from the law, but that which is through faith in Christ, the righteousness which is from God by faith* (Philippians 3:9). *Therefore, if anyone is in Christ, he is a new creation; old things have passed away; behold, all things have become new* (2 Corinthians 5:17). *I do not set aside the grace of God; for if righteousness comes through the law, then Christ died in vain* (Galatians 2:21).

Notice that, although in Galatians 2:21 above, God uses the word "righteousness," in 3:3 He uses the word "perfect" ....*Are you so foolish? Having begun in the Spirit, are you now being made perfect by the flesh.*

The Righteousness of God
Is the Perfection of God

God deposited, in us, his own perfection as our perfection!

"But," you say, "I'm not sinlessly perfect." That is true, however, your perfection does not come through perfect behavior. That, my friend, is the difference between law and grace. If you had not died with Christ, you would still be under a law system; you could work on your behavior for the rest of your life to become perfect—but you would never succeed. But under grace, perfection is not earned! It was given to you as a gift. Being a good Christian no longer depends on what you do, it depends on what you have and who you are! There is no longer a debate about who is a better Christian—one who prays before he eats, or one who prays before he puts gas in his car. We are one in Christ. His righteousness in me is equal to His righteousness in you, and vice versa, regardless of our respective behavior. There is no room for pride except in the Lord Jesus Christ, ...*as it is written, "He who glories, let him glory in the Lord* (1 Corinthians 1:31). I will repeat it: When he gave you his righteousness, he gave you his perfection, and now you are the righteousness (perfection) of God in Christ Jesus.

Become familiar with Hebrews 10:14. *For by one offering He has perfected for all time those who are sanctified.* You are perfect for all time. Don't be a dweeb, and say this is only true in God's sight! It must also be true in your own sight, or you will be falling into the Galatian error for the rest of your earthly life!

Chapter Four

Christians With a Law Mentality

Law and religion are in the same class:
they deal with externals;
hence they tend to hypocrisy, to a
covering up of the real heart condition.
One can act up to the Law's requirements
without being up to them.
Norman B. Harrison, D.D.

For a background to the title of this chapter, let us look at the legalistic Jews of Jesus' day. They insisted they did not need a new method of obtaining righteousness—they were satisfied with what they had. Jesus' new teaching presented a threat to them, just as it does today to those who are Christians in name but follow in the pattern of the legalistic Jews. Jesus' system of righteousness made him an offense to the Jews, *Behold, I lay in Zion a stumbling stone and rock of offense, And whoever believes on Him will not be put to shame* (Romans 9:33).

The old-time Jews appeared to have a good thing going. They had laws and standards by which they lived, and actually thought they scored quite well in their observances. If they did fail in any way, they would either re-codify, redefine the law in order to make it easier to meet its demands, or they would offer a sacrifice to provide a covering for their transgression.

The Gentiles, however, had no such forgiveness system. They recognized that works-righteousness, obtaining righteousness by cleaning up their thinking, feeling, choosing, and doing, was impossible. They were ready for a new system, a system based on faith instead of behavior. By faith in the finished work of Christ, resulting in the gift of life in Christ, they would be able to replace their own unrighteousness with the perfect righteousness of God. *What shall we say then? That Gentiles, who did not pursue righteousness, have attained to righteousness, even the righteousness of faith* (Romans 9:30).

In contrast, the legalistic Jews were satisfied with their human effort, thank you! They believed that, on the whole, they met the demands of law, so their works-righteousness, plus forgiveness, was satisfactory and they saw no need for a different system.

A Law Mentality

But God never intended for the law to be a means of obtaining righteousness, even for the Jew. For example, *Abraham believed God and it* (his faith) *was reckoned to him as righteousness* (Romans 4:3). The law, as a standard, was never intended to bring righteousness, but to lead people to Christ, who is our only source of righteousness, *....the law was our tutor to bring us to Christ, that we might be justified by faith* (Galatians 3:24). Sacrifices were only prescribed as a means of temporarily covering unrighteousness, not obtaining righteousness.

Today's Christians, who strive for righteousness under the law, aren't exactly like the legalistic Jews of Jesus' day. Today's Christian, with a law mentality, readily agrees that salvation is a free gift, received by faith in Christ alone. No true Christian believes in salvation by works.

However, there is little significant difference between the legalistic Jew and the law-minded Christian. For example....

The Legalistic Jew with a Law Mentality:	The Christian with a Law Mentality:
• Believed in God	• Believes in God
• Worked hard to do right	• Works hard to do right

• Lived by the law with God's help	• Lives by the law with God's help
• Sought to establish his own righteousness	• Seeks to establish his own righteousness
• Bragged of his righteousness	• Decries his unrighteousnes

The major difference between the two groups is that the legalistic Jew bragged of his ability to keep the law, while the law-minded Christian decries his inability to keep the law. Today's Christian loathes his unrighteous behavior, and his self-loathing looks like humility and spirituality! Rather than bragging about righteousness like the Jews of Jesus' day did, today's law-minded Christians look at their performance—their thoughts, behavior, choices, and feelings—and say, "Woe unto us; we are miserable wretches as Christians. Oh, but for God's continuous mercy and forgiveness, we would always be undone!"

What is wrong with this attitude, this belief system? Both the old legalist and the new legalist judge their righteousness, or lack thereof, by their behavior!

Today's Christian, whose circumcised heart has not yet been revealed, gets upset when we start talking about not being under law any more. He does not understand that the indwelling presence of Christ is sufficient to let us know right from wrong, so he clings in desperate dependence to the law that sets forth righteous behavior for him. "So what?" you say! God's plan was that we would obtain our righteousness apart from the law—as a free gift! *For if by the one man's offense death reigned through the one, much more those who receive abundance of grace and of the gift of righteousness will reign in life through the One, Jesus Christ.... Moreover the law entered that the offense might abound. But where sin abounded, grace abounded much more so that as sin reigned in death, even so grace might reign through righteousness to eternal life through Jesus Christ our Lord* (Romans 5:17, 20-21). God intended we would receive His righteousness as our righteousness in a faith transaction.

Christians and Law

You can easily identify a law-minded Christian. He gets nervous with verses like Hebrews 10:14, *For by one offering He has perfected for all time those who are sanctified.* He gets agitated when we affirm that Christ became sin so that we might become the righteousness of God in Him... (Note: One pastor at a men's retreat got very upset when I confessed that I was the righteousness of God. He felt few of us could make the same claim as Paul. I was supposed to be confessing my wretched sinfulness during the exercise.) The Apostle continued, *For He made Him who knew no sin to be sin for us, that we might become the righteousness of God in Him* (2 Corinthians 5:21). Clearly, we have become the righteousness of God in Christ!

A law-minded Christian is uncomfortable if he does not keep his gaze on evil thoughts, choices, actions, feelings. He measures himself by his performance, so he must work daily to rid himself of sin, in an effort to be assured that he is of value to himself or others. He feels guilty and shameful if he is not witnessing. His identity hinges on his self-righteousness and works-righteousness. He is on the opposite end of the behavior spectrum from the Pharisees.

Legalistic Christians give God credit for their better performances and blame themselves for their poorer performances. They regularly reduce themselves to tears as they promise God they will perform better, with his help. But, as Paul observes, *We know that the Law is good, if one uses it lawfully, realizing the fact that the law is not made for a righteous man (Christian), but for those who are lawless and rebellious, for the ungodly and sinners, for the unholy and profane, for those who kill their fathers or mothers, for murderers and immoral men and homosexuals and kidnappers and liars and perjurers and whatever else is contrary to sound teaching* (1 Timothy 1:8-10). In other words, the law was not made for Christians.

Those who look away from themselves and their performance for righteousness, glory in the righteousness God gave them as a gift by faith. *But of Him you are in Christ Jesus, who became for us wisdom from*

God—and righteousness and sanctification and redemption—that, as it is written, "He who glories, let him glory in the Lord" (1 Corinthians 1:30-31). They praise God for the gift that made them acceptable, worthy, pure, and holy in Christ Jesus.

For those who insist on living under law and look at their behavior for their righteousness—hear this warning! *But my righteous one shall live by faith; and if he shrinks back, my soul has no pleasure in him* (Hebrews 10:38).

Is it worth the risk of keeping a law mentality if it goes against what God desires of his children? Is it worth falling away from intimacy with Christ just to satisfy our need to add to what Christ accomplished for us? *You have become estranged from Christ, you who attempt to be justified by law; you have fallen from grace* (See Galatians 5:4.)

Do we want to experience God's pleasure? The glorious result of a grace mind-set is that our behavior will change for the good without the coercion of the law!

Chapter Five

The Mother of
All Obstacles to Grace

Man's basic characteristic is pride.
Its one antidote is Christ's humility,
ministered through the human channel
of lives humbly yielded to Him.
Norman B. Harrison, D.D.

Without exception, mankind has certainly been thick-headed or obtuse when it comes to the issue of pride. We have allowed neither history nor Scripture to loosen the binds of pride. In addition, there is a real shortage of press given to the subject of pride in the Christian community.

Grace Blocked

1 Peter 5:5-6 reads, *Likewise you younger people, sub-*

*mit yourselves to your elders. Yes, all of you be submis-
sive to one another, and be clothed with humility, for
'God resists the proud, but gives grace to the humble.'
Therefore humble yourselves under the mighty hand of
God, that He may exalt you in due time.*

These key verses point to several things.

- First, pride often manifests itself in rebellion against authority.
- Second, humility is demonstrated by subjection to authority.
- Third, humility is to pervade our relationships with one another in the church.
- Fourth, God's opposition to the proud, blocks his grace. Under the banner of God's unconditional love, we sometimes get the impression that God will not withhold his grace from anyone. However, God is opposed to the proud but gives grace to the humble.
- Fifth, God's grace is not handed out willy-nilly; there is a condition attached.
- Sixth, self-exaltation is out the window. With humility comes God's exaltation—in due time!

As ministers of grace, we must pay attention to these teachings. When people do not clearly understand the full message of grace, it is often because the problem of pride has not been addressed.

Slow Learners

There are innumerable references to pride and humility in the Bible. There are many stories that deal exclusively with the problem of pride. Lucifer and his underlings, were cast out of heaven due to his declaration of independence while being hell-bent to self-exaltation. *I will ascend into heaven, I will exalt my throne above the stars of God; I will also sit on the mount of the congregation, on the farthest sides of the north; I will ascend above the heights of the clouds, I will be like the Most High* (Isaiah 14:13-14).

Adam and Eve

Of course, Adam and Eve fell for the temptation to be like God, *For God knows that in the day you eat of it your eyes will be opened, and you will be like God, knowing good and evil* (Genesis 3:5). Certainly, this was an arrogance and authority problem.

Korah, Dathan and Abiram

Korah, Dathan and Abiram, who along with 250 leaders of the congregation, men of renown, gathered themselves together against Moses and Aaron saying... *You take too much upon yourselves, for all the congregation is holy, every one of them, and the Lord is among them.*

Why then do you exalt yourselves above the congregation of the Lord? (Numbers 16:3) In other words, there was a massive attempt, through the vehicle of self-exaltation, to usurp authority from God's anointed—Moses and Aaron.

Saul

Saul, the first king of Israel, disobeyed the Lord by disobeying Samuel the prophet, who told him to destroy the Amalekites and all living things among them. This execution was ordered by God because the Amalekites had repeatedly plundered the rear guard of the Israeli caravan during their exodus from Egypt. But Saul had a "better" idea; he determined to save the best of the animals and Agag the king. As he explained it to Samuel, *...the people spared the best of the sheep and the oxen, to sacrifice to the Lord your God...* (1 Samuel 15:15). Samuel's famous rebuttal followed, *Has the Lord as great a delight in burnt offerings and sacrifices, as in obeying the voice of the Lord? Behold, to obey is better than sacrifice, and to heed than the fat of rams. For rebellion is as the sin of witchcraft, and stubbornness is as iniquity and idolatry. Because you have rejected the word of the Lord, he also has rejected you from being king* (vv. 22-23).

Nebuchadnezzar

Nebuchadnezzar stood on top of his royal palace, and opened his royal mouth once too often with the royal words... *Is not this great Babylon, that I have built for a royal dwelling by my mighty power and for the honor of my majesty?* (Daniel 4:30). He asked this rhetorical question after being warned in a dream of what would happen if he did not rid himself of arrogance.

The Ramifications

Lucifer's fall, along with countless angels—now called demons—led to his opportunity to tempt Adam and Eve. Their fall led to sorrow, cursed ground, thorns and thistles, hard toil, sweat, separation of God and man, physical and everlasting death, sins of every kind, sickness, and infinite consequences for the human race.

Korah, Dathan, and Abiram's rebellion not only resulted in death for them and their families, but also for the 250 men of renown who were swallowed by the earth. When the congregation of Israel protested their fate and grumbled, 14,700 more people died of a plague.

Saul lost his kingdom, and a distressing spirit, sent from God, terrorized him the rest of his life... *But the Spirit of the Lord departed from Saul, and a distressing spirit from the Lord troubled him* (1 Samuel 16:14).

Saul's paranoia toward David, his successor, is well documented in the Scriptures; he lived out the rest of his reign in shame.

Nebuchadnezzar spent his next seven years crawling around as an animal in a pasture, driven from men, his body wet with dew, his hair like eagles' feathers and his nails like birds' claws, before he finally came to his senses. When next he opened his royal mouth he said, *Now I, Nebuchadnezzar, praise and extol and honor the King of heaven, all of whose works are truth, and His ways justice. And those who walk in pride he is able to put down* (Daniel 4:30-37).

Pride

Pride is a universal problem among men due to the results of the fall, which predetermined for each of us a birth in which we were separated from God. Because of this separation, it became necessary for each of us to meet our own needs, become god-players, live in self-sufficiency, and develop a strategy of living quite contrary to an abiding life in Christ. This incomplete and inadequate approach to life inevitably resulted in failure, with horrendous results.

Rather than facing our shame, we developed attitudes such as arrogance, rebellion, self-centeredness, self-reliance, self-protection, invincibility, and independence, all the while seeking power, influence and riches—all in an attempt to mask failure. Extreme examples of this strategy include such wicked men as, Adolph Hitler in Germany, Idi Amin in Uganda, Pol Pot in Cambodia, Saddam Hussein in Iraq, as well as other leaders. Each of these leader's pride determined their own particular race, tribe, or ethnic group was so superior that they had the right to eliminate others. In the United States, the national sense of superiority has even led to arrogant presidents whose terms ended in disgrace due to pride.

Pride has led to the failure of many famous Christian leaders. Pride has led to the rise of antichrists who have no need for God. Pride has led to arrogant conservatives and liberals alike, who advocate the usurping of God's appointed authority in the church. Pride has driven the controllers among us to reject and abuse others, in order to protect their supposed positions of superiority.

The Warnings

Even with all this historical documentation, God still patiently warns us in verse after verse:

> • Proverbs 16:5 *Everyone proud in heart is an abomination to the Lord; though they join forces, none will go unpunished.*
>
> • Proverbs 6:16-19 *These six things the Lord hates, yes, seven are an abomination to Him: A*

proud look, a lying tongue, hands that shed inno-cent blood, a heart that devises wicked plans, feet that are swift in running to evil, a false witness who speaks lies, and one who sows discord among brethren.

• Psalm 31:23 *Oh, love the Lord, all you His saints! For the Lord preserves the faithful, and fully repays the proud person.*

• Proverbs 16:18-19 *Pride goes before destruc-tion, and a haughty spirit before a fall. Better to be of a humble spirit with the lowly, than to divide the spoil with the proud.*

• James 4:6 *God resists the proud, but gives grace to the humble.*

• Proverbs 3:34 *Surely He scorns the scornful, but gives grace to the humble.*

Is there any doubt as to how significant this sin is among mankind? Is there not ample reason for God to detest this problem—even to the extent of withholding grace? Could it be that this transgression may be the real culprit behind many of the adversities we face in our individual lives, as well as in our families and churches?

Chapter Six

Fear, Anxiety, and Stress

Every adversity, every failure,
every heartache carries with it the seed
of an equal or greater benefit.
Napoleon Hill

Fear, anxiety, and stress prevent many Christians from experiencing joy, peace, and love in their lives. Thankfully, Scripture is clear about the solution to the fear, anxiety, and stress trifecta of trouble.

Over time, fear, anxiety, and stress are very destructive to the soul and body. Doctors are convinced that stress is linked to numerous physical and physiological complaints. It can effect, or exacerbate, sleeplessness, eating disorders, ulcers, high blood pressure, strokes, heart disease, and sexual dysfunction. It definitely affects many people's philosophies and theology.

Fear tempts people to do regrettable things. Fear can result in prolonged suffering in order to avoid death, betrayed friendships, lies, avoided martyrdom, perjury, even refusal to be seen with certain people.

Specific Fears

In counseling, I have identified certain specific fears that seem to stand out among the others. They are as follows and in no particular order:

- Fear of Failure
- Fear of Rejection
- Fear of Death
- Fear of Abandonment
- Fear of Loss

Fear of Failure

This is a very common fear that drives people to check and recheck their behavior. It often motivates people to hide mistakes. Fear of failure can be the motivation for distorting financial records, lying about achievements, and mis-leading investors.

The leader of a country must not fail in war. Jesus asked, *...what king, going to make war against another king, does not sit down first and consider whether he is able with ten thousand to meet him who comes against him with twenty thousand"* (Luke 14:31)? Failure in battle results in loss of territory, men and equipment, prestige, and sometimes even a country's existence.

Fear of failure is usually not an end in itself. 1 John 4:18 states, *...fear involves punishment (torment), and the one who fears is not perfected in love.* In other words, it usually does little good to ask people to stare failure in the face and try to figure out why they fear it. It is better to look elsewhere for the cause. However, I am not averse to helping people see that they are total failures in terms of the modus operandi of their first birth—which, of course, consists of flesh plus law. They are also failures because they lack the power of divine life, having been born spiritually dead. When we agree to be the total failures that we are under that operating system, the fear of failure can lose its power. My experience has been that when this decision is made, Christ reveals himself as our total success. He is a success.

Fear of Rejection

Behind the fear of failure is usually the fear of rejection. However, the fear of rejection becomes powerful because people do not know in an experiential way that they are acceptable. Once a person truly knows through revelation that he is acceptable to God, then he will be acceptable to himself, unless, of course, his view of what made him acceptable to himself is different than what made him acceptable to God. Rejection by men no longer holds power over those to whom acceptance is revealed by God.

But it does little good to tell a person that he is "accepted in the beloved" as noted in Ephesians 1:6, if acceptance is not experienced. And acceptance is not experienced when certain lies keep people working to make themselves acceptable.

What lies would those be? Take a moment and refer back to Chapter 3 – The Galatian Error where I emphasized the belief many hold that we are saved by grace, but made acceptable by works—thus my oft-repeated assertion that people commonly spend their entire Christian lives trying to become good Christians, in spite of Scriptures to the contrary. That is not to say that obedience isn't necessary as we will address in a later chapter.

Deceptions Which Hinder Acceptance

• "I am merely clothed in righteousness."
The truth is—in the New Covenant, I am indwelt by righteousness; it is part of who I am. *For He made Him who knew no sin to be sin for us, that we might become the righteousness of God in Him* (2 Corinthians 5:21). The often referred to "robe of righteousness" is Old Covenant, external, and rendered outdated by the New Covenant.

• "God doesn't really see me, He sees Christ in me."
The truth is—what scripture is this baloney based on?

• "God sees me as if I'm righteous."
The truth is—I am righteous! Why do we say "as if"? Does God really need to pretend that I am righteous? Does he put on his dark glasses to help in this pretension?

• "I'll be righteous when I get to heaven."
The truth is—this is true of my behavior, but not of my basic identity.

• "I'll become more righteous as I age, or as I mature."
The truth is—righteousness is received, not achieved. *For if by the one man's offense death reigned through the one, much more those who receive abundance of grace and of the gift of righteousness will reign in life through the One, Jesus Christ* (Romans 5:17).

• "I'm positionally righteous."
The truth is—the Bible teaches that righteousness is actual for the believer. *...just as He chose*

us in Him before the foundation of the world, that we should be holy and without blame before Him in love (Ephesians 1:4).

• "I'm righteous in Christ, but..."
The truth is—you can add anything you want to that sentence, and it will still be wrong!

• "I'm righteous due to the forgiveness of sins."
The reality that many people believe that forgiveness results in righteousness, is part and parcel of this deception.

Many people see their sins as being recorded on something like a whiteboard. If they commit ten sins on any one day, they are at a minus ten until they repent, confess, and are then forgiven.

Now that the whiteboard (their conscience) is clean, they are righteous until the next set of sins is committed and the process is repeated.

What is wrong with this thinking? Even if we are living on a continuous forgiveness system because of a misunderstanding of 1 John 1:9.... *If we confess our sins, He is faithful and just to forgive us our sins and to cleanse us from all unrighteousness, ...*this forgiveness cleanses us from unrighteousness, but it does not give us righteousness. Thus, the minus ten, after forgiveness brings us to zero.

We need to be in the infinite plus column but this approach will not give us righteousness. Righteousness is not given on the basis of the forgiveness of sins, but is the gift of Christ himself.

Until the believer accepts the righteousness of Christ as his very own, by faith in the Word of God, he will forever see himself as though he is apart from Christ, unacceptable, unworthy—a poor, wretched sinner, saved by grace. This system of false beliefs will cause him to struggle for acceptance.

The precious words, "in Christ Jesus," are scattered generously throughout the epistles. Until the Holy Spirit reveals to us who we are "in Christ Jesus"— united to Him, one with Him, joined to Him, immersed in Him, in union with Him—we will forever see ourselves only as ourselves in separation from Christ. We will consequently fear failure and rejection.

Why? Because, without that revelation, we have not been "perfected in love" ...*There is no fear in love; but perfect love casts out fear, because fear involves torment. But he who fears has not been made perfect in love* (1 John 4:18). Thus, we will not see ourselves as loved!

In reality, how lovable are we? As lovable as we are acceptable. How acceptable are we? We are one with Him, so if he is acceptable, then we are acceptable! If we know God, we know love. If we know Christ, we know ourselves. The weapons of failure and rejection lose their power.

Fear of Death

There are people who live every day fearing the walk through the valley of the shadow of death. Some people have good reason to fear death, because they have no sure evidence of where they will end up. Garrison Keillor (the humorist) once told a story of a man who had married several times, leaving a trail of women and children behind. Keillor said this man left instructions that, upon his death, his remains were to be cremated, and his ashes scattered over the ocean. Keillor's take on this was the guy wanted to make it hard for God to find him!

Death represents a loss of control. Many people falsely believe that they have not lived one day of their lives out of control. Control mechanisms can only prevent death to a point. For example, we can do things to help prevent heart attacks, but they are not guaranteed to work. We might be able to control diet, but we cannot control stray bullets, drunken drivers, misdiagnoses, terrorist attacks, school shootings, hurricanes, aneurisms, and other tragedies and diseases beyond our limited power.

People have an illusion that they can control their lives, and it terrifies them to think they need to give up all rights to what happens to them in a presentation of themselves to the Lord. Implied in such a presentation is the willingness to be obedient to God and his delegated authorities. One must give up all rights to what happens to him, and become willing to give thanks in all things without figuring out why! *I beseech you therefore, brethren, by the mercies of God, that you present your bodies a living sacrifice, holy, acceptable to God, which is your reasonable service. And do not be conformed to this world, but be transformed by the renewing of your mind, that you may prove what is that good and acceptable and perfect will of God* (Romans 12:1-2). Then, and only then, will Christ fill us with his presence, eliminating fear of death and subjection to this bondage. *...through death He might destroy him who had the power of death, that is, the devil* (Hebrews 2:14). Destroy here means, "render ineffective" or "render powerless." Peace and calm are in Christ.

The idea that we can control what happens in our lives, in such a way as to prevent death, is an illusion. We are not omniscient, therefore, we have a need to surrender to the one who is omniscient, omnipresent, and omnipotent. He alone can keep us in safety if he pleases.

To eliminate the fear of death, the believer must make a conscious decision to trust God. He must violate his natural inclination to stablilize his life before he abandons himself to God. Waiting is intended to guarantee he will never need to make a full surrender.

When the peace comes, the believer will find that

71

God had no desire to control him after all, but merely wanted to set him free from the tyranny of self-sufficiency. God himself has no desire to make a believer a puppet, but rather to break self's rule and enable the Christian to become obedient to the Spirit voluntarily. Only then can God protect us and only then will we want to obey Him.

John 5:24 has long been a comforting verse to me... *Truly, truly, I say to you, he who hears My word, and believes Him who sent Me, has eternal life, and does not come into judgment, but has passed out of death into life.*

I find two comforting thoughts in this verse. First, the believer will not be judged, except for good works. We are judgment-exempt, because the perfect track record of Jesus Christ is substituted for our track record when his righteousness became ours. Second, the only death we will ever experience is past tense. We were dead in Adam. Believers have eternal life. Eternal life cannot and will not die. The life we have— His life—will always live. We need not fear death, because we don't die. Our body merely drops off! How good is that? *And this is the testimony: that God has given us eternal life, and this life is in His Son. He who has the Son has life; he who does not have the Son of God does not have life* (1 John 5:11-12).

Fear of Abandonment

This fear too is based on false premises. We will never find the lie causing this fear if we do not allow the Holy Spirit to take us through the terrorizing feelings of abandonment, to the ultimate source of the lie's power. I must make a decision to let abandonment happen, to find out what is on the other side of this fear. When we discover the lie and quit using fleshly means to keep abandonment from happening, Christ will show up as our life-source, causing this fear to disappear.

The fear of abandonment often stems from abandonment by significant people during one's childhood. It can also arise from growing up in families who threaten to remove love, support, and security if certain conditions are not met. Pride may prevent the person who is threatened from succumbing to such manipulation, but the emotional damage is done. Anger, however, can be a camouflage, hiding the true source of pain. When the anger is dealt with, the source of the fear may be exposed.

Fear of Loss

Loss can come in many forms. It can hit our financial portfolios, our relationships, our health, our prestige, and our position at work. We will see how much power such things have held over us when we observe how we react to their loss.

Those of us who teach the cross and the life see over and over again that loss is the way of the cross.* Luke 9:23-25 gives us this statement from our Lord: *"If anyone wishes to come after Me, let him deny himself, and take up his cross daily and follow Me. For whoever wishes to save his life will lose it, but whoever loses his life for My sake, he is the one who will save it. For what is a man profited if he gains the whole world, and loses or forfeits himself?"*

Many times God uses loss to show us our false gods, impure motives, pointless goals, hollow securities and "broken cisterns." *For My people have committed two evils: They have forsaken Me, the fountain of living waters, and hewn themselves cisterns—broken cisterns that can hold no water* (Jeremiah 2:13).

How we react to the loss will reveal whether or not we are broken cisterns. For example, if the loss of a farm causes an identity crisis (I don't know who I am anymore), then God has exposed a problem. If the loss of a loved one sends us into a seven-year depression, we might be missing the circumstances God has used to enable us to discover who our treasure is.

* When I mention the cross, I am distinguishing the work of the cross from the work of the blood of Christ. The cross is a means of execution, of death, whereas the blood is an instrument of cleansing and forgiveness. When we experience the cross, we have our death with Christ made real in our experience.

When Jesus told us the cost of discipleship, he also told us our first birth relationship needed to be sanctified in order to experience our new relationship in Christ. *"If anyone comes to Me and does not hate his father and mother, wife and children, brothers and sisters, yes, and his own life also, he cannot be My disciple. And whoever does not bear his cross and come after Me cannot be My disciple"* (Luke 14:26-27). Is discipleship worth this risk? Will Jesus really provide a better love in the exchange of life?

Discovering Where Our Treasure Is

There are several causes of depression. Although the majority of depressions are due to the insufficiency of self-sufficiency and the missing power of Christ in both the carnal Christian and the non-Christian, there are organic issues that can affect people as well. There are bipolar disorders which are often attributed to lithium imbalances. Post Traumatic Stress Disorders present difficult journeys for military people. Hormonal imbalances can cause organically based depressions.

Although medications can be useful for many depressions, it is important to check if the person seeking help has experienced the cross. It is my experience that although the majority of Christians know the work of the blood of Christ experientially, very few have experienced the cross.

There is a saying many grace life counselors use: "Stress plus time will reveal your functional source of life!" When loss is looked at in this perspective, it can be an encouragement in the midst of the pain. When our false source of life is revealed, confessed, and abandoned, Christ, through prayer, will reveal Himself.

That is the goal, and it puts an end to the fears!

Chapter Seven

Identity Theft

Religion survives because it answers
three questions that every reflective person must ask.
Who am I?
Why am I here? How then shall I live?
Jonathan Sacks

The older I get, the more I become aware of the damage inflicted on mankind by Adam and Eve. We were made aware as children of the obvious and painful things like work, death, illness and disease. Later we found out about more problems like flesh, the world system, demons, principalities, and darkness. We also see birth defects, sexual disorientations, false philosophies, religions of men, political powers, etc. Now, in my senior mindset, I want to focus on one more kind of damage inflicted on us: identity theft.

I am somewhat naïve regarding the ways of con

artists who steal identities. Unfortunately, large businesses must have people engaged full-time in security matters to protect them from viruses, identity theft, stolen trade secrets, copyrights and patents. Even a small ministry like ours has to hire people to protect us from internet theft, invasion of our web site, theft of bank accounts, loss of social security numbers, and computer viruses. Yes, even the protection of our reputation itself.

The Original Identity Theft

Lucifer wanted to steal God's identity when he—a beautiful, created being—aspired to be like God. However, God would have none of it, and booted him out of heaven. On earth he conspired to kidnap the human race, steal our identities, and cause most of mankind to search for the rest of their lives to reclaim their identity. Unfortunately, once the damage was done, few even knew they needed a new identity, let alone an identity that could be received, rather than achieved.

After Nebuchadnezzar besieged Jerusalem and captured the sons of Judah—young men with no blemishes, good-looking, gifted and intelligent—he was brazen in his attempt to change their identities. He simply changed their names. Daniel, Hananiah, Mishael, and Azariah became Beteshazzar, Shadrach, Meshach and Abednego. Their nrew names all honored Babylonian gods. As a child I referred to these new names without thinking about the implications of identity change. Today I see the treachery of it all. Their new Chaldean names were designed to cause them to forget who they truly were: children of Israel—beloved of God.

Kidnapping

People, especially impressionable young people, can be influenced by kidnappers. Recently a young teen was kidnapped from a strong Mormon family by a couple who were crazed polygamists. It was not long before they had her convinced that her parents were not searching for her, so they must not love her. She was told that God had chosen her to be a wife for the shiftless, homeless drifter who had kidnapped her.

Stories like this abound about children who, for example, are kidnapped by a divorced parent who wants sole custody, but can't get it in the courts. The children are told that their custodial parents didn't want them anymore, or had asked the kidnapping parents to take them. The children are brainwashed to think if their parents loved them, they would come after them; certainly they would search for them. Isolated from the news and the truth, the children begin to believe the lies.

The Method

The technique of stealing and recreating identities is intended to destroy or distort a person's true history and origin. Start by telling lies about parents and loved ones, proceed by changing their name, and finally isolate them from anyone who might speak the truth. This tactic was first employed by the evil one when he instituted his plan in the Garden. He has infiltrated the church with lies and works to make certain that our temporary identities, based on law and flesh, are deeply ingrained. The enemy continues to lie to us about God. Satan has even given us many false leads about the way to God. Thus, when Jesus said he was the Way, the Truth and the Life, he was looked upon with skepticism—and he still is!

Although our true identity was never consummated in the Garden of Eden (because we didn't partake of the tree of Life), our potential for identity in Christ and union with Christ was always there. Once our original parents fell for the lie, the revelation of our potential identity in Christ Jesus had to be postponed for thousands of years. God raised up the nation of Israel to keep their shattered identity somewhat alive for thousands of years. He called them his people, and even identified himself by their ancestral fathers by saying, "I am the God of Abraham, Isaac, and Jacob." He was not ready to reveal himself through the Christ, until the fullness of time had come. He revealed himself as the God who was the restorer of true identity for the human race. Unfortunately, *He came to His own, and His own did not receive Him* (John 1:11).

But some received him, *....as many as received Him, to them He gave the right to become children of God* (John 1:12). We, the kidnap victims found our true identity as children of God when we came to Christ. By receiving us into the family of God, and by being joined to him, he has made us one with him... *But he who is joined to the Lord is one spirit with Him* (1 Cor. 6:17). He, in an instant, changed our names from sinners to saints. He changed us from being the unrighteous to being the righteous, *for He made Him who knew no sin to be sin for us, that we might become the righteousness of God in Him* (2 Cor. 5:21). He ransomed his own, and made us children of God. He now calls us *...a chosen generation, a royal priesthood, a holy nation, His own special people* (1 Peter 2:9). He says that we *...once were not a people but are now the people of God, who had not obtained mercy but now have obtained mercy* (1 Peter 2:10).

How Our Name is Changed

Again and again the Jews called the Gentiles sinners during the Old Covenant period. They even suggested Jesus was a sinner. Christ dined and talked with sinners and said he came to save sinners. The Pharisees thought Gentiles to be inferior for their failure to keep the law as the Jews did.

After Christ ascended into heaven the epistles made a distinction between believers and unbelievers as you can see in the following.

Law	Grace
Convicted and identified you by your behavior; thus you are what you do!	Identifies you by the person of Christ; thus you are who you are in Christ!
• If you lie, you are a liar.	• If he is righteous, I am righteous.
• If you steal, you are a thief.	• If he is holy, I am holy.
• If you murder, you are a murderer.	• If he is acceptable, I am acceptable

You can see that for Paul to refer to himself as a sinner, it is likely he was referring to his pre-Christian days. At that time he says he was guilty of putting Christians in prison and voted for their death... *many of the saints I shut up in prison, having received authority from the chief priests; and when they were put to death, I cast my vote against them. And I punished them often in every synagogue and compelled them to blaspheme; and being exceedingly enraged against them, I perse-*

cuted them even to foreign cities (Acts 26:10-11). In 1 Timothy 1:13, Paul refers to himself as formerly a blasphemer, a persecutor, and an insolent man.

His shame apparently led him to believe that up until his salvation, he was the chief of sinners. Praise the Lord that Paul found that the grace of our Lord was exceedingly abundant through his faith and love for Christ Jesus.

How necessary it was for us to die to the law which labels us under the former covenant!

The Theft Continues

Unfortunately, there are those who still lie to us concerning our identities. Those who mislead and deceive us are mainly confused people of God. They want us to compromise our recovered identities. They encourage us to base our identities on our behavior rather than on who we are in Christ Jesus. These false identities sound reasonable to us, but they are really lies. They sound something like this:

• Don't call yourself a saint… that has to be earned by years of hard labor and certain confirming miracles. Rather call yourself a forgiven sinner, or a sinner saved by grace. That is much more humble.

• Don't call yourself righteous. That might get confused with self-righteousness, and we don't want to sound proud.

• Forget that you have received the free gift of God's righteousness in Christ Himself. *...if by the one man's offense death reigned through the one, much more those who receive abundance of grace and of the gift of righteousness will reign in life through the One, Jesus Christ* (Romans 5:17).

• Above all, never quote Hebrews 10:14, *For by one offering He has perfected forever those who are sanctified.* Why? Because we Christians shouldn't use the word perfection. Rather, say that you are becoming a better and better Christian sinner as you try hard, with God's help, over an 80 year life span. In this we confuse maturity with identity. Perhaps the father of lies has deceived us in this area more than any other.

If we believe the lies, then we might as well act as though we are still kidnapped, and try to establish a new identity through our own efforts at becoming a better and better Christian (sinner).

Part 2

The Solution

Chapter Eight

Saved By His Life

"Saved by his life!" His holiness,
his righteousness, his truth....
saved now and in the future by and in
Christ's risen life which we now share.
William R. Newell

One of the great treasures we have is the book, *The Saving Life of Christ*, by Major Ian Thomas. This incredible man has founded Torchbearer centers around the world. Young men and women from around the world attend these schools for the purpose of being discipled by one of the Major's leadership teams.

In his book, Major Thomas tells the story of how he came to grasp the truth that we are saved by Christ's life. After describing seven years of doing everything he could to serve Christ, but only becoming utterly exhausted spiritually, he says:

"...I got down on my knees before God, and I just wept in sheer despair. I said, 'Oh, God, I know that I am saved. I love Jesus Christ. I am perfectly convinced that I am converted. With all my heart I have wanted to serve Thee. I have tried to my uttermost and I am a hopeless failure!' That night things happened.

"I can honestly say that I had never once heard from the lips of men the message that came to me then ... but God that night simply focused upon me the Bible message of Christ who is our Life ... The Lord seemed to make plain to me that night, through my tears of bitterness: 'You see, for seven years, with utmost sincerity, you have been trying to live for Me, on My behalf, the life that I have been waiting for seven years to live through you.'

"I got up the next morning to an entirely different Christian life, but I want to emphasize this: I had not received one iota more than I had already had for seven years!"

I suppose it is possible Christians would have noticed, sooner or later, they aren't saved by Christ's death, but Thomas' book certainly makes clear what Romans 5:10 states so plainly ... *we were reconciled to God through the death of His Son, much more, having been reconciled, we shall be saved by His life.*

Not Only Major Thomas

The truth of being saved by his life is one that escaped me for most of my life. If you had given me a quiz, asking me what I was trusting in for my salvation, my answers would have been any of the following: my beliefs, my faith, Christ's death for me, the blood of Christ, the fact that I'm forgiven, etc. Others, who followed church traditions rather than the Scriptures, might have added baptism, church membership, or living a life of love and concern for others.

Certainly believing is necessary for salvation, however, believing in itself is not sufficient for salvation. As James, the Lord's brother, indicated in verse 2:19... *even the demons believe, and tremble!* The Scripture does say... *Believe on the Lord Jesus Christ, and you will be saved* (Acts 16:31), however, God never intended for us to trust in our ability to believe. It was God's intent for us to emphasize the one in whom we believe—the Lord Jesus Christ. Believing is an activity of the mind, but salvation takes place in the spirit as we partake of divine life.

Faith is a necessary ingredient of salvation. *For by grace you have been saved through faith...* (Ephesians 2:8). However, faith alone is not what saves us. If we believe we were born dead (separated from God), and that Christ died for us in order to remove our sins (reconciliation), so that he could give his life to us (salvation), then it certainly makes sense to ask him to give us his life. That very decision is an act of faith. But faith, in this sense, is an activity of the will, just as believing is a function of the mind.

Many claim they are trusting in Christ's death for salvation. Certainly, without Christ's substitutionary death for us we could not be saved. This final sacrifice was necessary to divert the wrath of God from us to the innocent Lamb who was made sin for us. Furthermore, as Romans 5:10 reads... *We were reconciled to God through the death of His Son.* We were reconciled because the source of our enmity with God was removed, i.e. our sins. Thus Christ's death on the cross reconciled us to God according to the Scripture; but his death is not what saves us.

Still others trust exclusively in the blood of Christ to save them. Many songs reinforce the idea that we are saved by the blood. It is true that the blood cleansed us from our sins, redeemed us, and gained our access to the Father. But while the blood of Christ has tremendous significance in the process of salvation, it is not ultimately what saves us.

There are many fine Christians who trust in confession and forgiveness for their salvation. They worry they will not enter Heaven if they do not have all their sins confessed up to date. They believe in a cleansing based on a sin-by-sin confession. Thus for example, if someone commits suicide, he cannot possibly enter Heaven, because there is no time for confession after the suicide mission is completed. So they are really trusting in an up-to-date cleansing and confession resulting in forgiveness for salvation, which of course then depends partly on works, i.e. the work of confession. The common misunderstanding of 1 John 1:9, leads to such erroneous thinking. (See Chapter 14)

For if when we were enemies we were reconciled to God through the death of His Son, much more, having been reconciled, we shall be saved by His life. Romans 5:10 is clear that none of these responses should be trusted in for our salvation. For most of my life, I would not have been able to say that it is his life that saves me.

What was our basic birth defect at salvation? Ephesians 2:1 tells us, *....we were dead in trespasses and sins.* What do dead people need more than anything else? Life, of course! Thus when Christ died in our place and shed his blood for our sins, he removed the only obstacles keeping us from partaking of divine life. In other words, he had to give his life for us before he could give his life to us! The death of Christ was not an end in itself; it was a means to an end. After all, wasn't it he who said... *I came that they might have life, and might have it abundantly* (John 10:10)?

I fully realize that many Christians are taught Christ gave his life for us in order that we could be forgiven and go to Heaven when we die. Although that is true, it is not the complete salvation story.

So many gospel messages are impotent today, at least in part, because of an incomplete presentation of the salvation message. Jesus did not say, "I have come that you might have forgiveness and have it abundantly." He wanted to be united to us; to be intimate with us; to be one with us. That is why He said... *I have come that they may have life!* That is why his desire for oneness was repeatedly included in his teaching, *....that they all may be one, as You, Father, are in Me, and I in You; that they also may be one in Us* (John 17:21).

Let me challenge you to be one of the very few Christians who unashamedly say, "I am saved by his life!"

Chapter Nine

The Finished
Work of Christ

"It is finished!" Everything necessary
for the putting away of the sins of His people,
providing for them a perfect standing before God,
and fitting them for it, had all been done.
Arthur W. Pink

The longer we walk the Christian journey, the more desperate we become for that which satisfies, frees, and gives us greater peace.

One of my favorite questions for people is this, "Being totally honest, is there any way in which you are disappointed with Christianity as you know it?"

Many refuse to admit they are disappointed, but sometimes a brave soul will admit Christianity has been a hardship; lacking in peace, tranquility, rest, joy, and love.

Why is this? Is it because of striving, faulty beliefs, false teaching or corrupted concepts of God? Yes! But more likely it is because of an incomplete understanding of the finished work of Christ.

One of the ways in which the finished work of Christ is minimized has to do with conquering the devil and all his ways. Christians today have no problem believing Christ has provided the solution for sin in terms of forgiveness, but it's quite another matter to believe the Christian has no role in achieving victory over temptations, or "besetting sins", as some ancients liked to call them. We often hear, "I need to ask Christ to conquer my addiction, lusts, and sinful passions," or, "I must conquer these temptations with God's help." This reasoning seems so right. However, it is so wrong!

In addressing this issue we need to remind ourselves ....*The words and promises of the Lord are pure words, like silver refined in an earthen furnace, purified seven times over* (Psalm 12:6 Ampl). God means what he says and although translations often use different words in an effort to clarify what God is saying to the reader, paraphrases have often done more harm than good. Consider for example, the following terms:

• old nature: this term is not a Biblical expression but is commonly used in error as a substitute for the real Biblical words "old man."

• sin nature: this too is not a Biblical expression but was invented to define the words "old man" or possibly "the flesh."

• <u>old sin nature</u>: probably an invention to substitute for "old man."

• <u>old man</u>: defined below.

• <u>old self:</u> the old man. Old self is not a strict translation but it is used in the NASB, RSV, Amplified, and NIV versions.

• <u>sinful nature:</u> a non-Biblical expression unfortunately coined by the NIV translators to designate the flesh.

• <u>flesh:</u> this is a Biblical term explained below.

• <u>human nature</u>: a term describing the nature of humanity.

• <u>lower nature:</u> a non-Biblical term which adds to the confusion.

• <u>power of sin:</u> a force or power which is in us, but not us as described in Romans 6, 7, and 8.

• <u>sin:</u> either used to refer to the power of temptation in Romans 6-8 or to describe violations of the law.

• <u>in the spirit</u>: refers to a Christian who is in Christ.

• <u>in the flesh:</u> refers to a non-Christian and is a similar term to being in Adam.

• <u>after the flesh:</u> refers to actions of a person who walks after, or according to, the flesh. This is a Biblical phrase.

• <u>after the Spirit:</u> refers to actions of a person

who walks after, or according to, the Holy Spirit.

This too, however, is a biblical phrase.

One pastor took offense when I told him that the word of God is done a disservice when these terms are used interchangeably. He told me that, "peas, corn, carrots, and broccoli may be different vegetables, but really they are all forms of the same thing." So really, all apples, of course, are fruit. But not all fruit are apples.

The New International Version (NIV) for example, has no problem using old self for the Greek word meaning old man, sinful self for the word flesh, plus other words which are used by the enemy to confuse the saints who study the scriptures. Is it any wonder Christians have difficulty in discovering what Paul wants us to understand about victory over sin in Romans 6? Is it any wonder when people are counseled on how sin is conquered they are taught, coached, and discipled to use primarily human effort? (See Appendix E)

As you study Appendix E you will see a brief description of the words that pertain to Romans 6-8. In Appendix F you will see a graph showing our possible positions and our possible conditions (experiences) as well as our walk. If you carefully note the prepositions, you will see how meticulous the apostle Paul wrote his letter to the Romans. Please do not gloss over these descriptions, because they will enable you to understand Romans 8 and other sections of the Bible. For example, you will never again refer to yourself, a Christian, as being in the flesh. On the other hand, you as a Christian can walk after the flesh or after the Spirit. Only non-Christians are in the flesh. Furthermore, they can only walk after the flesh.

More than a conqueror

To bring clarity, let me simplify the teachings on this subject by using strict translations of the Greek words in an effort to offer a clearer look at what Paul wants us to know about our victory over sin.

The apostle wants us to be fully informed of how God views the "old man," which we believe to be the "unregenerate man," or "unregenerate spirit." The phrase "old man" is only referenced three times in the New Testament. Each time, when translated correctly, it is said to be crucified. Therefore it is not the enemy most Christians say it is when they refer to the "old man" or the "old sin nature" as their enemy.

The strict translation of the Greek word "sarx" is the word "flesh." In simple terms, we refer to it as the self-sufficiency of man as he functions apart from Christ. The flesh can be understood in a multitude of other ways in the Bible, but we use this common understanding of it.

Another word we need to better understand is sin.

This word is sometimes used as a "power" and sometimes as an "action." In Romans 6, 7, and 8, it refers to a power (a source of temptation) which is in me, but not me! Notice, for example, Paul's statement... *But now, it is no longer I who do it, but sin that dwells in me* (Romans 7:17).

The non-Christian is of Adam and thus is, or has, as his identity, the "old man." Because of this, sin is his master and the non-Christian is a slave to sin's power. He has no divine life indwelling him and thus has only his own resources and the law to keep him from doing evil. (See Appendix C)

As an illustration it is like a Roman soldier taking a person captive and putting a ring in the man's nose, to which a chain is attached. If the slave is tied to the soldier for the rest of his life but is then executed and born anew he would be free. However, if he had the same mind and memory system as when he was a slave, he might never believe and enjoy his new freedom.

Similarly, when the old man was crucified with Christ, at the time a person becomes a Christian, that person was released from sin's power over him: *....knowing this, that our old man was crucified with Him, that the body might be released from sin's power so that we should no longer be slaves of sin. For he who has died has been freed from sin. Now if we died with Christ, we believe that we shall also live with Him, knowing that*

Christ, having been raised from the dead, dies no more. Death no longer has dominion over Him. For the death that He died, He died to sin once for all; but the life that He lives, He lives to God. (Romans 6:6-10).

This co-crucifixion with Christ means that the new Christian died to the law, to sin (as a power), and to the world. *Therefore, my brethren, you also have become dead to the law through the body of Christ, that you may be married to another—to Him who was raised from the dead, that we should bear fruit to God ....But now we have been delivered from the law, having died to what we were held by, so that we should serve in the newness of the Spirit and not in the oldness of the letter* (Romans 7:4 and 6). *Therefore, if you died with Christ from the basic principles of the world, why, as though living in the world, do you subject yourselves to regulations* (Colossians 2:20). And, as noted in Romans 6:7, *"he who has died has been freed from sin."*

The Bible is not saying that we died to our sins, but rather that we died to Satan, the world, and to sin *as a power*. Romans 6:11 tells us... *Likewise you also, reckon yourselves to be dead indeed to sin, but alive to God in Christ Jesus our Lord.*

If Christ's way of dealing with temptation was to die to it, and to include us in His death, what makes us think we can have an alternate way of dealing with temptation by striving, scratching, clawing, groaning and moaning to overcome it as though victory is something we must achieve because Christ failed to over-come it. This is blasphemy! It is a denial of the finished work of Christ!

Let me be clear. The enemy did not lose his power. But he did lose his power *over us.* We also came alive through Christ's resurrected life, and the life we now live by faith, is already victorious over our enemies. Again, this in no way implies Satan does not have power to persecute and oppress Christians. Indeed, there continue to be many who die for their faith at the hands of evil ones. Rather, that he lost his power *to make us sin.* If we sin now, it's because we choose to sin! I am not suggesting that we died to our sins (actions), rather, I am stating that we died to the enslaving powers of sin, Satan, and the world.

The Reality of "Victory"

It should be clear that our life in Christ does not become more victorious. It is already victorious, and striving will do nothing to make it more victorious than it is. You might say, "I don't feel victorious, nor do I have a track record of demonstrating victory." The victorious life of Christ is not subject to proving his victory by your feelings, nor is he interested in your need to confirm his power by your track record. You only need to look at the Scriptures to find what is true about your relationship to Satan, sin, and the world.

The old man is not the Christian's problem. Deception is the problem. The old man lived in self-sufficiency, but now the Christian has a choice. He can live as though he is self-sufficient, or he can live in Christ's sufficiency. It all depends on whether he chooses to live according to the flesh (self-sufficiency), or according to the Spirit (Christ's sufficiency). This is why abiding in Christ or the vine is so important for the believer (see Romans 8).

As a friend noted about this truth, "....your relationship to your enemies is the same relationship that Christ has to them. Look away from yourself, and evaluate what is true and what is possible by the indwelling life and power of Christ!"

To pray for victory over temptation is an affront to the finished work of Christ. To pray for more power or strength, is to minimize the gift of resurrection life we already possess. To believe that I can add to the victory Christ accomplished at Calvary is to deny his triumph and to make myself the conquering hero instead of him.

In Paul's letter to the Ephesians, he tells Christians he prays that the eyes of their understanding might be opened to the fact that the power which raised Christ from the dead, is now in them. Not only did God raise Christ from the dead, but he seated him at his own right hand, ...*far above all principality and power and might and dominion, and every name that is named, not only in this age but also in that which is to come. And He put all things under His feet, and gave Him to be head over all things to the church* (Ephesians 1:21). In the next chapter Paul again reminds us of where we reside because God has, *....raised us up together, and made us sit together in the heavenly places in Christ Jesus* (Ephesians 2:6).

The passage clearly tells us that we are in Christ Jesus, in the heavenly places. Are we therefore not far above all power, principality, might, dominion, and every name that is named, not only in this age but also in the age to come? Of course, we are! As you seek to apply this truth to your understanding, take the time to meditate on the full passage, Ephesians 1:19-2:7.

Christian... do you have any problem believing that you were in Adam, and therefore what happened to Adam happened to you? No? Then why would you have a problem believing that you are spiritually in Christ and what happened to Christ happened to you?

What Now of Temptation?

As you set your mind on your position in Christ, are you in victory or still struggling for victory? When you face temptations, do you thank the Lord that they were conquered more than 2,000 years ago when you were in Christ at the cross? Or do you ask for more strength, power, or help, and a support group to assist you?

Most of us were taught to achieve our own victory over sin and to fight to overcome such things as lust, gluttony, lovelessness, pride, lying and many other sins. We are seldom, if ever, told ....*to put to death your members which are on the earth: fornication, uncleanness, passion, evil desire and covetousness, which is idolatry* (Colossians 3:5). Verses 8 and 9 tell us we can put off all these: *anger, wrath, malice, blasphemy, filthy language out of your mouth. Do not lie to one another since you have put off the old man with his deeds.* If we must fight to overcome these temptations, Christ did not conquer them at the cross when we were in him. We have been taught that we need to add our self-effort to what he failed to complete in his cross, resurrection and enthronement. Yet, self-effort results in promises we will certainly fail to keep.

God has always had a plan to join us to Christ. His original plan was to join us to himself by inviting us to eat of the tree of life in the Garden of Eden. When we failed to take advantage of this plan, God brought forth his plan of joining us to Christ through his resurrected indwelling life. By our union with his life we are now made acceptable and complete—holy and without blemish. Will we now live by the invisible part of us, by faith? Or will we put our faith in the visible realm—including our emotions?

It all has to do with the finished work of Christ! Is it a plan that is sufficiently victorious? Or must we work to

make ourselves more victorious every day of our life?
God forbid!

Chapter Ten

Deception in the Garden

The man whom God created
was indeed good, but there remained
a deciding issue—that of life and death.
Watchman Nee

The damage in the Garden of Eden was of momentous proportions. The damage was far greater than many believed. The consequences included more than instant spiritual death and progressive physical death. The tree of life represented Christ's life. Man was created to be a container, a vessel, and a dwelling place for the Most High. After the deception, humanity would have to wait till after the Cross to receive Christ's life. Mankind's new propensity for sin would bring with it pain, sickness, disease, aging, and endless work for the newly formed rebels.

The disobedience, manifested by eating of the forbidden tree of the knowledge of good and evil, was universally disastrous. After sinning, man became self-sufficient in his own eyes, separated from God, and forbidden from eating of the Tree of Life. Man had thwarted the great master plan of God to give man his Spirit to indwell him and live life in him and through him. Sin had forced man to live in a way God never intended for man to live out of his own resources.

Centuries later a mystery would be revealed to the Apostle Paul—a happening, a momentous reclamation project that was never possible for Old Testament believers. This wonderful revelation, made possible by the work of the Lord Jesus, was that Christ would come to live in us—the hope of Glory! *God willed to make known what are the riches of the glory of this mystery among the Gentiles: which is Christ in you, the hope of glory* (Colossians 1:27).

Why was this separation from God such a disaster? What was so bad about Adam and his descendents functioning out of self-sufficiency—independence and separation from God? Didn't they have all it took to live life successfully on the earth? They had souls consisting of a mind, a will, and emotions, and they had bodies with five senses and the functions of speech and action.

The terrible consequence of separation from God was incompletion. Their human spirits, their innermost parts, were without the abundant life God had created them to enjoy. Humanity was like a lamp without oil, a car without fuel. They were running on only two of eight cylinders.

Birth Defect

The incompleteness, or birth defect, comes standard in every descendent of Adam and Eve. Pediatricians can't spot it in babies, teachers seldom know about it in the classrooms, and parents struggle to identify it, however, it is a defect present in every person born into this world.

Dogs, cats, and other creatures God made have all of their body parts with eyes, ears, nose, lungs, and heart. If the other organs work well, they are pronounced normal! Normal for creatures mentioned above means they are whole and complete. It's easy to jump to the reasonable conclusion that man is created whole and complete as well. Not so! Normalcy for mankind is incompleteness, without divine life. It results in self-sufficiency. It means being weaker and less clever than Lucifer and his hosts because God is not in us. He is outside of us.

Heed this carefully, if God's great plan was that he would live his life in us, for us, and manifest his son Jesus Christ through us, then when his Son is absent from us, do you expect we should be able to handle the pressures of life? The pressure of this fallen world, the stress, the temptations, the hurt, the pain, the grief are impossible to deal with without divine life.

If God designed us in such a way that he would be our divine source of life, but due to his absence we had to rely upon our own resources, do you think depression would be normal or abnormal? Would anxiety be normal or abnormal? How about captivity, bondage, failure, and sin? All these things would be normal not abnormal! And yet, because the world does not know that we are all born abnormal with a birth defect, without a supernatural life, it has diagnosed all of the above as sickness and disease. The conclusion is that man's inability to function well is due to bad circumstances, lack of opportunity, complications due to childhood separations, inadequate solutions, poor self-esteem, environmental stresses, bad fortune, and a lack of self-discipline.

Granted, our circumstances are often difficult, complicating the inability of the self-sufficient, but the number one problem you and I had at our entrance into this world was a birth defect! We were incomplete, without hope, and without God.... *you were without Christ, being aliens from the commonwealth of Israel and strangers from the covenants of promise, having no hope and without God in the world* (Ephesians 2:12).

Therefore, the Christian should be thinking that the abnormal is normal, and the normal is abnormal. Is it any wonder that those who advocate the popular descriptive phrase of co-dependency believe 90% of all people are co-dependent.

The mistake they make of course, is not understanding that 100% of all people are co-dependent in their first birth. We all came into the dysfunctional world, having dysfunctional parents from the first family on down because we were all born incomplete: with a birth defect.

A Greater Deception

We of course expect the world to be deceived. We expect them to not know normality from abnormality, good from evil, or light from darkness. But why in heaven's name is most of the church ignorant of this? Why does the Christian community buy into all the insanity of calling non-physically-based mental, emotional, and relational symptoms sickness instead of normalcy, or the works of the flesh, which is how the Bible describes them? Let me suggest it's because the same effects of self-sufficiency and incompleteness afflict the church. How can this be? Isn't the Christian indwelt by the Holy Spirit? Of course! But if the person is indeed a Christian isn't he complete? Remember, I mentioned earlier that Christians have the same difficulties in their ranks as the world does. The Christian community is not hearing how God came to free us from who we are in our first birth. We aren't being taught how to exchange our source of life.

The church is hearing that God came to set them free from what they have done—forgiveness for their sinful past. In the meantime, they are left to struggle and fight the good fight to set themselves free, and to overcome and cope with the bondage, the captivities, the destructive personalities, and their past. God, they are told, will help them do this.

The truth of the matter is that the gospel of forgiveness is not enough, and neither is the gospel of trying to produce the fruit of the Spirit with God's help.

The Set-up

We learn at a young age the need for a life based on self-sufficiency. We were born self-centered, self-sufficient, self-empowered, self-actualized, and self-protective. If we were going to be somebody, we had to be self-made. If we were to find freedom from dependency we had to work to become independent. If we were going to improve our image, we had to develop self-esteem. These traits are looked upon as worthy goals.

Somewhere in the process we hopefully invited Christ into our life. We were told that Christ came to help us. Help us—the self-sufficient, independent ones—to live the Christian life, to help us to defeat sin and temptation, to help us cope with the stresses of life, and to not only help us but to strengthen us and guide us as well.

Consider, for example, the vine and the branches Jesus spoke of in the gospel of John. Can you imagine the branches on a vine being asked what role the vine plays in their life, and answering "Well, the vine came to help me be a good branch. The vine came to be my assistant. I am quite capable of being self-sufficient except when times get tough. Then I need to ask the vine for help. However, be assured that I give the vine credit for everything I do."

The vine would say, "Oh foolish branch, apart from me you are dead and have no life. I am your very life, your identity, your source of power. You bear fruit because of me! Apart from me you can do nothing. Get over your arrogance, your pride, your self-sufficiency. And, by the way, self-exaltation is another of your problems."

It is a deception that God came to be our helper, rather than our life. Certain scriptures of course, refer to the Holy Spirit as our helper, or comforter, as in the following, ...*so we may boldly say: "The Lord is my helper; I will not fear. What can man do to me?"* (Hebrews 13:6). These are largely quotes from the Old Testament when God was outside of man instead of indwelling man. He never intended that the Holy Spirit would help the flesh to be self-sufficient and self-loving. They are opposed to one another. *For the flesh lusts against the Spirit, and the Spirit against the flesh; and these are contrary to one another, so that you do not do the things that you wish* (Galatians 5:17).

Flesh Enablers

The underlying issue is we have not been taught to exchange our original strategy for living at birth—the self-sufficient life—for the Christ-sufficient or dependent life. However, we have been taught to improve the flesh. More often than not, our Christian teachers have been flesh enablers.

Of course, there are many variations of this deception for Christians. Many think that abiding in Christ is the flesh depending on Christ when performing a particular task.

I personally opted for the throne concept for five years. When I sinned, I believed self was on the throne. When I confessed every known sin and asked to be controlled by the Spirit, I claimed Christ was on the throne. Let me explain.

He Came to be My Life

I in no way wish to detract from the kingship of Christ, but the throne concept masks a deeper truth. Jesus Christ didn't come to be on the throne of *my* life! He came to be my life! *When Christ who is our life appears, then you also will appear with Him in glory* (Colossians 3:4), *I came to give life—life in all its fullness (John 10:10 NCV)*, and.... *For to me, to live is Christ* (Philippians 1:21). When he is experienced as life, he will also be my Lord and King.

The two trees in the Garden of Eden symbolize the following:

Tree of the knowledge of good and evil	**Tree of LIFE**

Flesh	Spirit
Independence	Dependence
Bondage	Freedom
Law	Grace
Death	Life

When people function in the insufficiency of self-sufficiency, trusting Christ to be their helper rather than their life, they function as though they are complete. All the while they continue to be self-managed (in moderation), self-improved, self-motivated, self-willed, self-actualized, self-protective, and self-loving. They try to measure up to God's expectations by not being lovers of self, but it is impossible not to be what they are—self-sufficient.

The reason man has trouble distinguishng which tree he is eating from is because he has three choices—good, evil, and Life. The good produced by the flesh can easily be mistaken as the fruit of the Spirit.

Chapter Eleven

The Exaltation

As a branch of Christ the Vine,
you are merely a channel
for the flow of His life.
Think of yourself as such. Live as such.
Norman B. Harrison, D.D.

When I ask someone in counseling, "Have you received your exaltation yet?" people usually respond by asking what that looks like. Obviously, I can't answer that question, because it was different, for example, for Nebuchadnezzar than it was for Jesus. I do believe that someone who has been exalted will know it and won't have to ask what it looks like.

Our exaltation may not be granted immediately. The Scripture says it will be ours in due time. Job's exaltation took time as God replaced his flocks and material things. We know his latter days were blessed more than his beginning days with twice as much live-stock as he had prior to his trials. *Now the Lord blessed the latter days of Job more than his beginning; for he had fourteen thousand sheep, six thousand camels, one thousand yoke of oxen, and one thousand female donkeys. He also had seven sons and three daughters* (Job 42:12-13).

Exaltation Takes Different Forms

Jesus' exaltation was different from Job's. Jesus, *humbled Himself and became obedient to the point of death, even the death of the cross. Therefore God also has highly exalted Him and given Him the name which is above every name, that at the name of Jesus every knee should bow, of those in heaven, and of those on earth, and of those under the earth, and that every tongue should confess that Jesus Christ is Lord, to the glory of God the Father* (Philippians 2:8-11). Lest we protest, "But that was Jesus," God reminds us... *Let this mind be in you which was also in Christ Jesus... Therefore work out your salvation with fear and trembling* (Philippians 2:5,12). He is definitely referring to the subject of humility and exaltation as it unfolds in our experience.

Nebuchadnezzar's exaltation came after seven years in a pasture. His understanding was returned to him, and he broke out in praise and adoration to God. This happened without medications for schizophrenia or inpatient hospital care. Next he says, *....for the glory of my kingdom, my honor and splendor returned to me. My counselors and nobles resorted to me, I was restored to my kingdom, and excellent majesty was added to me* (Daniel 4:36).

A Modern-Day Example

In June of 1982, Bill McCartney was hired as the head football coach at the University of Colorado. Having served under Bo Schembechler at the University of Michigan, he seemed well-groomed to reverse the pathetic woes of the Buffaloes. Shortly after he arrived, the Buffs lost to Kansas State. The loss was an embarrassing moment for the team, because in those days no team of any significance lost to K State!

In February of '86, Coach McCartney recruited a Samoan, Sal Aunese, to quarterback the Buffaloes. By October of that year, the long-suffering CU fans were rewarded with a win over the Nebraska Cornhuskers. This kind of triumph had not happened for 20 years! But tough times were coming for the McCartney family. Bill and Lyndi's daughter Kristi told her parents in June of 1988 that she was pregnant; the baby's father was Sal Aunese. To add to the pain, Sal wanted nothing more to do with Kristi.

Bill and Lyndi reacted to their daughter's pain with hurt, but also with support. Lyndi wrote an incredible letter to Sal, not condemning him, but encouraging him in his football career. Her heart reached out to Sal.

In March of 1989, the football squad was wracked with the devastating news that Sal Aunese had cancer, an incurable kind that almost always was fatal. In April, little Timothy Chase was born to Kristi. Sal wanted nothing to do with Kristi, but did want to see the baby.

In spite of all their hurt and woundedness, the McCartneys refused to reject Sal! In fact, on July 12, as Sal lay desperately ill on a hospital bed, Bill McCartney led Sal to the Lord.

The enemies of Life and Truth then went to work. Westword, a scandal paper in Denver, published an article designed to inflict great injury on the McCartneys. They showed a caricature of coach McCartney with a crown of thorns on his head. Surrounding him were four devilish creatures representing his players, mocking him. The article went on to make fun of his faith and the morals of Kristi, who was, of course, crushed by the article.

In September Sal Aunese died. Five thousand dignitaries, government officials, and students attended the memorial service in Colorado. At this service, Bill McCartney manifested once again his humility and his support for his daughter. He said, "Kristi McCartney, you've been a trooper. You could have had an abortion, or gone away and had the baby someplace else to avoid the shame. But you didn't. You stayed here.

You're gonna raise that little guy, and all of us are gonna have the opportunity to watch him. It looks like we've got another lefthander coming up in the ranks. Kristy, I admire you. I respect you. I love you so much."

Angry letters flowed to Bill from abortion proponents. But there were also letters of support from women and young girls from around the nation, because of how he supported his daughter in her great need. Contrast McCartney's approach with those parents who, while protecting the family pride, heaped shame and rejection on their daughters in their hour of greatest need. The McCartneys proved their humility, and God honored them.

A Trip to the Orange Bowl

On January 1, 1990 the University of Colorado beat Notre Dame in the Orange Bowl and the CU Buffaloes became national champions. Coach McCartney was directed by God to raise up *Promise Keepers,* a ministry that has impacted tens of thousands of men. The McCartneys humbled themselves; and in fulfillment of God's promise, he exalted them in due time.

A Humility Checkup

It's time to ask ourselves some questions. Is self-righteousness getting in the way of experiencing the righteousness of God? Do we give God credit for our achievements, while we secretly glory in ourselves? Are those of us with titles serving those under us, or do we insist on being served? Do we embrace humility, or do we maintain face and save our pride at any cost? Can we say with Job, *Though He slay me, yet will I trust Him* (Job 13:15)?

Moses was a man about whom God said, *Now the man Moses was very humble, more than all men who were on the face of the earth* (Numbers 12:3).

The prophet Micah wrote, *He has shown you, O man, what is good; and what does the Lord require of you but to do justly, to love mercy, and to walk humbly with your God?* (Micah 6:8). Isaiah wrote, *But on this one will I look: on him who is poor and of a contrite spirit, and who trembles at My word* (Isaiah 66:2).

Let this be our final thought: It is our job to humble ourselves under the mighty hand of God. You can trust Him to provide the circumstances. Also leave it to him to work out the why, how, and when of our exaltation.

—For additional information about the McCartneys, see his book, *From Ashes to Glory*, Thomas Nelson Publishers, 1990.

Chapter Twelve

Is Behavior Important?

To be in Christ—
that changes your destination;
but for Christ to be in you—
that changes your destiny!
Major W. Ian Thomas

The Bible does tell us to pay attention to behavior. In Colossians 3 we are told to consider ourselves dead to *....immorality, impurity, passion, evil desire, and greed, which is idolatry.* We are also told to put off.... *anger, wrath, slander, and abusive speech from your mouth. Do not lie to one another, since you put off the old man with its evil practices.*

We often buy into the idea that many of the things listed require experts, such as an addictions counselor to help with various forms of addictions. But aren't these really immoralities, impurities, passions, evil desires, and greed?

Addictions are seen as a form of helplessness, but why are Christians helpless? Isn't it non-Christians who are supposed to be helpless or enslaved? Romans 6:17-18 states, *But thanks be to God, that though you were slaves of sin (past tense), you became obedient from the heart to that form of teaching to which you were committed, and have been freed from sin, you became slaves of righteousness.*

How then can a Christian be addicted? Because of lies that are believed, including the lie that righteousness is achieved. It is a chain reaction.

One possible scenario might read like this: Jack is highly desirous of receiving acceptance and approval from his parents who are Christians. They are very critical of people, however, and Jack finds that nothing he does is good enough. A grade of B should have been an A. A triple should have been a home run. If he weren't so clumsy he wouldn't have tipped over his milk. If he were a true Christian, he wouldn't want to watch R-rated movies.

As Jack grows up, he learns that he cannot perform well enough for others, let alone himself. When he goes away to college, he finally is able to do what he thinks he wants to do: party, drink, and chase girls. His first year of college is a disaster. His therapist says he was so beaten up while growing up that he is reacting situationally to the constant attacks on his psyche by escaping into riotous living.

What are the issues for Jack? Must he simply change his behavior? His attitudes? Since he grew up in a Christian home, certainly he knows what is right and wrong, doesn't he? Does he simply need to put off the bad behaviors and put on the right behaviors?

I think we all agree that the life story of Jack is common. Parents like to see their kids perform well. So does God. If kids look good then their parents look good, and they can take great pride in their kids while appearing nonchalant about it. Therefore parents threaten, harangue, and criticize their kids, and as Bill Gillham says, "try to stomp the ignorance out of them."

The fact of the matter is, we all have been "Jack" to some degree. When Jack's parents evaluated his performance, focusing on his imperfections, they were doing what comes naturally—raising Jack under a law system.

There was only one way to evaluate his behavior, attitudes, choices, and actions—that was to have standards in mind when they evaluated him. Thus the standard they used included Albert Einstein when it came to smarts, Barry Bonds when it came to slugging baseballs, Emily Post when it came to manners, and a multitude of other worldly stars. His parents, of course, ignored their own shortcomings, or, when confronted with their mistakes, they would say "That's different," for whatever reason. That is why Paul was rather sarcastic in Romans chapter 2 when, in verses 17-24, he pokes fun at those who think they are a cut above the others because they are good law-keepers, and they sit in judgment on those who are not. *Indeed you are called a Jew, and rest on the law, and make your boast in God, and know His will, and approve the things that are excellent, being instructed out of the law, and are confident that you yourself are a guide to the blind, a light to those who are in darkness, an instructor of the foolish, a teacher of babes, having the form of knowledge and truth in the law. You, therefore, who teach another, do you not teach yourself? You who preach that a man should not steal, do you steal? You who say, "Do not commit adultery," do you commit adultery? You who abhor idols, do you rob temples? You who make your boast in the law, do you dishonor God through breaking the law? For "the name of God is blasphemed among the Gentiles because of you," as it is written.*

I am not saying that unacceptable behavior should be thought of as acceptable.

The point is, we won't be able to change our behavior until we obtain our acceptance and love in a way unrelated to our performance. Not only was Jack's behavior not good enough to please his parents, but he also knew that his acceptance by them was dependent on his performance.

The New Covenant

There are two major results of the finished work of Christ that if accepted as gifts and believed will transform Jack's life. The first is related to acceptance, and the second is related to victory. The latter truth is somewhat more difficult to understand and will be much easier to understand if you refer to Appendices C, D, and E. They will require study, but they represent marvelous truths, which if understood will change your understanding in how to deal with temptation forever. The truths of Romans 6, 7, and 8 will be easier to understand. Also, as you visualize how the Bible has carefully defined terms, together with Christ's complete setting of the prisoners free, you will rejoice forever.

New Covenant Acceptance

First let us uncover Jack's unshakable acceptance. The good news is that God comes to us and makes us acceptable totally independent of our performance. How? He simply changes the basis by which we become acceptable to Him. Rather than requiring us to change our behavior, attitudes, and feelings in order to be acceptable, he graciously forgives us for everything we ever did wrong up until the time we were born again, and then gives us his righteous life to make us acceptable forever. In other words, he comes to us with a completely different operating system than what we grew up under!

In essence, God says to the person operating in rebellion, like Jack, "Jack, I know you never performed well enough to please the adults in your life, and therefore you never found the love and acceptance for which you searched. Finally, you gave up and became licentious, rebellious, angry and insolent. Let me offer you a whole different plan. I will give you as a free gift, my absolute righteousness, which will now be your perfection. No longer should you think that you don't measure up to my standards, because you have become the righteousness of God and I find no fault with you." Jack replies, "What about my behavior and attitudes?" God says, "Your behavior is now irrelevant to your righteous identity. You are a slave partaker of my divine perfection, and you can do nothing to change that. I will no longer judge you by what you do, but by what you have." Jack then says, "Then I guess the reason for my rebellion has vanished," and God says, "You got it." Look closely again at how Paul expressed this, ...*God be thanked that though you were slaves of sin, yet you obeyed from the heart that form of doctrine to which you were delivered. And having been set free from sin, you became slaves of righteousness* (Romans 6:17-18).

In Romans 10:4, the Bible reads, ...*Christ is the end*

of the law for righteousness for everyone who believes. This means that God no longer looks at performance to determine righteousness for the Christian.

Now that Jack finds himself acceptable to God, what if he still doesn't find himself acceptable to man? This will likely be the case. We can't glibly say it doesn't matter, because it does matter that some of us will never be acceptable to our parents or to others around us. It is still going to hurt, but it need no longer control us. When Jack truly accepts his acceptance—his perfection in Christ—he will no longer be controlled by his quest for love and acceptance or his rage, feelings of despair and hopelessness. Rather he will operate out of fullness, love and gratitude. Now his behavior can change.

New Covenant Victory

So does behavior matter as Christians? Yes, because the Bible says that for those who operate as rebels, *....the name of God is blasphemed among the Gentiles because of you* (Romans 2:24). God cares what kind of behavior non-Christians see in us. They will think that becoming a Christian has no relevance for living if they don't see something different in us.

Behavior also matters for us. *Do you not know that when you present yourselves to someone as slaves for obedience, you are slaves of the one whom you obey, either of sin resulting in death, or of obedience resulting in righteousness* (Romans 6:16).

This is the time to study Appendix B, C, and D. It is so necessary to have some kind of concepts in our mind in order to live according to Gods word. For example if you do not know the difference between the old man and the new man, you will believe the lie perpetrated by most Christians that we have two identities. If we are both old man and new man, part of us is condemned and part of us is righteous; part of us is in Christ, and part of us in Adam; part of us is saved and part of us is unsaved; part of us is going to heaven and part of us is going to hell! We are both sinners and saints because we buy into the idea that when the old man is forgiven, it makes us a new creation. Which part of you do you identify with?

However the diagrams show us that the old man was crucified with Christ. Because sin as a power needed the old man to make us a slave, we are freed! When God crucified the old man, and replaced him with a new man, the new believer was set free from his slavery to sin. Similarly, if a horse is set free from his bridle and reins, the horse is set free from his owner. He can voluntarily obey his owner, but he can also obey a new master and disobey his owners.

When the slaves were set free through the emancipation proclamation, it took two years for some of them to hear the news. Therefore slave owners continued to treat their slaves the same old way, taking advantage of their ignorance. The death of the old man is our emancipation proclamation but the devil attempts to deceive us that we need to fight for our freedom. In this way we attempt to duplicate the finished work of Christ. Unfortunately, most churches tell you that your old man is not dead. They use biblical language when they tell you to fight the fight of faith. In reality however, they are telling you to fight the fight of works! This teaching is tragic and deceitful. How God must weep that his son's painful sacrifice is wasted!

Jack must be taught two truths after he becomes a Christian; his acceptance and his victory.

Destruction will come into our lives if we live in disobedience to God. We give Satan access to us when we forsake the shelter afforded by staying under God's umbrella of authority. We stay protected when we live under his authority which in turn protects us from spiritual attack levied by principalities, powers, darknesses, and demons in the unseen world. Just look around at your world. Destruction resulting from rebellion and disobedience is all around us.

Chapter Thirteen

The Christian's Bar of Soap

I like your Christ,
I do not like your Christians.
Your Christians are so unlike your Christ.
Mahatma Gandhi

First John 1:9 is often referred to as "the Christian's bar of soap," and with good reason. Many people have taken this verse as being addressed to Christians. Thus, when they get entangled in sin, they believe that if they simply confess and ask for forgiveness, God will then indeed forgive them, and cleanse them from all unrighteousness. After all, the verse reads as follows... *If we confess our sins, He is faithful and righteous to forgive us our sins and to cleanse us from all unrighteousness.* For many years I have questioned how this verse is applied, because if it is used in the traditional way as described above, many other verses in the Bible appear to be inaccurate or untrue.

Early Memories

I remember the early teachings in my home and church. A normal morning worship service would include the reading of the Law of God from Exodus 20. We were told that we needed to hear the Law in order to come under conviction of our many grievous sins from the previous week. It was also necessary to hear the Law in order to learn how to live.

After reading the Law to us, the pastor would confess to God all of our likely sins that came into his mind. He would decry our lack of gratitude, neglect of the Word, failure to pray without ceasing, evil thoughts, and whatever else came to mind. By this time in the service, I was pretty well convinced that I was rotten to the core! Then, because we were under a great deal of conviction due to our "continuous sinning in thought, word, and deed," he would proceed to read 1 John 1:9. The preacher would then pray a corporate prayer on our behalf, pleading for forgiveness. Once we had confessed (or he had confessed for us), we were ready to sing a song of gratitude. The song would be one that drew our attention to the forgiveness that God had once again given us, like He did for David in Psalm 51. If the pastor didn't want to take the time to tell God all our sins, due to time constraints or other pressures, he could simply catch them all by referring to them as our "sins of omission and commission". When we had captured the whole of our combined sins, we were announced to be cleansed and up-to-date in forgiveness.

If the sermon could be structured in such a way that the preacher could "really sock it to us" because of our depravity, we had plenty to talk about after church. Somehow we all felt better when we were corporately nabbed by this man of God who was speaking on God's behalf. We had been found out again, and the condemning sermon would be referred to as a "really good sermon". If the preacher could make us cringe a bit, "he was doing his job". That was what preachers were for, after all—to keep us on our toes, cleansed, forgiven, and sin-free.

My early memories are of this constant battle to fight sin. It was a pretty hopeless task, however, because even the great Apostle Paul had struggled with it. Didn't he refer to it in Romans 7, when he told us that he was always doing things he shouldn't do and not doing things he should? Therefore we didn't have to feel wretched alone, because if Paul couldn't live the Christian life, then we shouldn't expect to be able to either. Every prayer I remember hearing from my parents and other adults ended with the phrase "and forgive us for all our sins." There, we had done it! We had cleared our record, and we were forgiven again. Never mind that we hadn't confessed any sins by name in preparation for that ending sentence. All that mattered is we had asked to be forgiven. There you have it. That was how we did it!

Problems

Not too long into my adult life, I became aware of problems in this approach. What if I deliberately sinned, could I be forgiven? What if I forgot to confess a particular sin; would I still be forgiven? What if I didn't truly repent? How would I know if I were truly repentant? What if a person committed suicide as a Christian? And could the verse just as easily read, "If I don't confess my sins, He is faithful and righteous to forgive me my sins and cleanse me from all unrighteousness?"

I recognize that using 1 John 1:9 as a verse for Christians has given many people comfort. People seem to feel a need to deal with sin by confession and asking for forgiveness. I remember the days when I used the verse this way in counseling Christians. I would also refer them to 1 John 1:7, where the apostle said, ...*if we walk in the light as He Himself is in the light, we have fellowship with one another, and the blood of Jesus His Son cleanses us from all (every) sin.* Thus, I could reassure people that there is no sin from which they could not be forgiven, even after they became Christians, because the Apostle John used the word "all." This was of great comfort to those who had been hiding secret, dark, defiling sins.

There was another problem. Christ died for all our sins, before we were even born. Thus we conclude that, when we were born again, God forgave all our sins, past, present and future. Therefore, if Christ died for all our sins, even before they were actually committed in time and space, why do we still need to obtain forgiveness after we become Christians by exercising the message of 1 John 1:9? It would seem that we should already be forgiven, shouldn't we? Or did Christ only forgive us for the sins we had committed up until the time we became Christians, leaving us the need to obtain forgiveness, one by one, for the sins committed after we became Christians?

Actually, this need not be a problem, experts told me. "It isn't that God hasn't forgiven us. It is just that we won't experience that forgiveness until we confess and accept that forgiveness on a sin-by-sin basis. God sees us as forgiven, right from the start of our Christian life," they said. "That is positional truth. Experiential truth won't come until we agree with God on a sin-by-sin basis."

However, there are verses in the gospels that seem to indicate that forgiveness is conditional upon my correct responses. For example, *....his master was angry, and delivered him to the torturers until he should pay all that was due to him. "So My heavenly Father also will do to you if each of you, from his heart, does not for-*

give his brother his trespasses (Matthew 18:34-35). This verse indicates that if I don't forgive my brother from the heart, God is going to turn me over to the tormentors (jailers) until I pay all my debts. Another example is in the The Lord's Prayer which requests God to forgive us our debts as we forgive our debtors. Wow! What if I don't forgive all my debtors? Will I be in trouble?

Verses Incompatible With 1 John 1:9

There are many verses that seem to indicate my sins are totally and completely forgiven by virtue of my being in Christ Jesus. Ephesians 1:7 reads, In Him we have redemption through His blood, the forgiveness of our trespasses, according to the riches of His grace. Colossians 1:14 reads, In whom we have redemption, the forgiveness of sins. Both of these verses say forgiveness is already ours, and there are no conditions attached, except that we need to be "in Him." Ephesians 4:32 reads, Be kind to one another, tenderhearted, forgiving each other, just as God in Christ also has forgiven you. Again, forgiveness is past tense. Even in 1 John 2:12 we read, ...your sins are forgiven you for His name's sake. Is there any doubt that this forgiveness is past tense?

Forgiven....or not?

I believe the teachers and preachers who tell us that the Bible calls for us to obtain repeated forgiveness after each sin, both of omission and commission, are neglecting vast portions of the Word of God. This kind of teaching often leads to a lack of assurance of salvation for example. I recall the admonition of a pastor father to his son when he said, "Son, make sure that, once you become a Christian, you never sin again. But if you do, be certain that you have time to confess the sin before you die and/or the Lord comes back, because otherwise you will go to hell." This young pastor could never find assurance of salvation because he continually was worried about dying with unconfessed sin in his life.

My son once attended a wedding where the pastor concluded the ceremony by asking for forgiveness for all the grievous sins we had committed. Immediately after the wedding the reception was held in the church basement. An elder began the reception by opening in prayer. At the conclusion of his prayer, he asked the Lord to "forgive us for all the grievous sins we had committed." My son wondered what grievous sins had been committed in the stairwell in the short time it took them to go from the sanctuary to the basement.

The Big Three

A lady I counseled told me that she grew up in a strict fundamentalist church. She said the big three sins which could cause her to lose her salvation if Jesus came back while she was engaged in any one of them, were dancing, playing cards, and attending movies.

Her aunt, who believed this teaching, gave her a strategy whereby she could attend a movie. She told her to sit on the end near an exit. Then, if Jesus returned, she could quickly scramble out of there, confess her sin, and still make it to heaven.

The Lutheran Approach

Finally, I wish to state my admiration and thankfulness for Martin Luther, for his brave revolutionary role in the Reformation, at the risk of death.

Yet, as with many reformers, his followers have not progressed nearly enough in appropriating the finished work of Christ. And, the Lutherans are not alone. In many of their churches when the sacrament is given, the following ritual is observed:

> *O almighty God, merciful Father, I, a poor, miserable sinner, confess unto Thee all my sins and iniquities with which I have ever offended Thee and justly deserved Thy temporal and*

eternal punishment. But I am heartily sorry for them and sincerely repent of them, and I pray Thee of Thy boundless mercy and for the sake of the holy, innocent, bitter sufferings and death of Thy beloved Son, Jesus Christ, to be gracious and merciful to me, a poor, sinful being.

Then the Minister shall pronounce Absolution.

Upon this your confession, I, by virtue of my office, as a called and ordained servant of the Word, announce the grace of God unto all of you, and in the stead and by the command of my Lord Jesus Christ, I forgive you all your sins in the name of the Father and of the Son and of the Holy Ghost.

A ------- men!

————Taken from a book of Lutheran liturgy.

I trust you agree the doctrine of forgiveness can be confusing. In listening to students, I find many living in fear, many living in confusion, and many never resolving the paradoxes in scripture on this topic. Can clergy forgive people on God's behalf? Is it a useful tool of legalism to do such things—to require public forgiveness of adultery as a warning to others?

We can't cover all scenarios on this, but I believe the next chapter will erase much of the confusion.

Chapter Fourteen

A Deeper Look
at First John

Confession is good for the soul
only in the sense that a tweed coat
is good for dandruff—
it is a palliative rather than a remedy.
Peter De Vries

The problem we wish to consider now includes these facts:

> 1) there are several verses which indicate that forgiveness is completed at the point of placement of the believer in Christ Jesus.
> 2) these verses make no mention of further need of appropriation of forgiveness.

Points of View

Three considerations are made by respected teachers:
1) 1 John 1:9 is merely referring to the need for confession and forgiveness by God for restoration of fellowship with God and one another, not for salvation.
2) The apostle uses the word "we" over and over; thus he must be talking about Christians in the church.
3) 1 John 2:1 is definitely addressed to Christians, *My little children, these things I write to you, so that you may not sin. And if anyone sins, we have an Advocate with the Father, Jesus Christ the Righteous.* Therefore 1 John 1 must also be written to Christians.

All these considerations seem formidable as we address the issue further. Nevertheless, I firmly believe that he is not addressing Christians alone in chapter one, and this is very important to understand.

Solution

In the second chapter of First John, beginning in verse 18, we find much enlightenment for our predicament. Read this carefully and thoughtfully. *Little children, it is the last hour; and as you have heard that the Antichrist is coming, even now many antichrists have come, by which we know that it is the last hour. They went out from us, but they were not of us; for if they had been of us, they would have continued with us; but they went out that they might be made manifest, that none of them were of us. But you have an anointing from the Holy One, and you know all things. I have not written to you because you do not know the truth, but because you know it, and that no lie is of the truth. Who is a liar but he who denies that Jesus is the Christ? He is antichrist who denies the Father and the Son. Whoever denies the Son does not have the Father either; He who acknowledges the Son has the Father also.*

Do you notice how many of the mysteries of the first chapter are answered in these verses? John is addressing what had become an intolerable situation in the church. People who did not believe that Christ was God had somehow obtained entrance, and perhaps membership, in the local body. I could envision that these antichrists may have joined the local church because it was a relatively new phenomenon; or perhaps these were people looking for relationships, or social gatherings; or perhaps it was the newest thing to do. Maybe notable dignitaries, artists, teachers, or local politicians were joining the church, so others did as well. I don't think it would be improper to think that these people enjoyed the potlucks, the picnics, the children's programs, the concerts or whatever was the custom at the time. For all we know, the church could have attracted the local youth by including a teen hangout. Perhaps the young people of the antichrists were dating the young people of the believers, and they all cruised their DUVs (donkey utility vehicles) through town. We do not know how many people were numbered in this group, but there were enough to make quite a stir!

At some point, however, it became apparent that there were significant differences between the belief systems of the truly saved and those of the antichrists. Now I doubt that these people were called by the name "antichrists" at the time. I think they were people along for the ride, who enjoyed the fun and activities of this phenomenon called "church." The apostle identifies them as antichrists in this letter.

When people leave the church, anger, frustration, and unhappiness often result. Some blame the pastor, others point to the requirements of membership or the lack of programs, and still others blame things like doctrinal stands. Perhaps some in the church had been influenced by the antichrists and said that they could still maintain fellowship with these people, even if they didn't want any part of Christ. Thus we see why John used the editorial "we" in addressing the problems left in the wake of these people leaving the church. He is addressing not only the antichrists who left, but also those influenced by them, and he makes many points of truth that cannot be compromised.

In verse 1, he tells them all that Christ was indeed God, because he and the other apostles heard him, saw him, and even touched the Word of Life.

That which was from the beginning, which we have heard, which we have seen with our eyes, which we have looked upon, and our hands have handled, concerning the Word of life.

In verse 2, he said the Christ was eternal life itself, and He had been with the Father before He entered our world.

....the life was manifested, and we have seen, and bear witness, and declare to you that eternal life which was with the Father and was manifested to us

In verse 3, he states that the church would like for the antichrists to reconsider their position, both because they wanted to have fellowship with them and because, if the antichrists changed their position to conform to truth, they could have fellowship with the Father and the Son.

....that which we have seen and heard we declare to you, that you also may have fellowship with us; and truly our fellowship is with the Father and with His Son Jesus Christ.

In verse 4, John wanted those who went out to have joy.

And these things we write to you that your joy may be full.

In verse 5, he declares that light does not characterize the life of those who left, but they can have light if they are willing to be placed in Him.

> *This is the message which we have heard from Him and declare to you, that God is light and in Him is no darkness at all.*

In Verse 6, people who say they have fellowship with Christ, and yet deny His deity and entrance into the world, lie and do not practice truth.

> *If we say that we have fellowship with Him, and walk in darkness, we lie and do not practice the truth.*

In verse 7, walking in the light results in mutual fellowship and also results in cleansing of all sin.

> *But if we walk in the light as He is in the light, we have fellowship with one another, and the blood of Jesus Christ His Son cleanses us from all sin.*

In verse 8, do you actually believe that any person can even become a Christian if he says he has no sin? John makes clear that such nonsense means the truth is not in us.

> *....if we say we have no sin, we deceive ourselves and the truth is not in us.* The truth is Jesus Christ.

In verse 9 in the light of this, isn't it reasonable that John is making his appeal in verse 9 to the antichrists. In other words, if you get honest with the facts of who Christ is, what He did, and what your real problem is, you too can become Christians by confessing your sins, and God will forgive and cleanse you.

> *If we* (the editorial we) *confess our sins, He is faithful and just to forgive us our sins and to cleanse us from all unrighteousness.*

In verse 10, he says such wild beliefs mean such a person calls God a liar, and again His word is not in such people.

> *If we say that we have not sinned, we make Him a liar, and His word is not in us.*

I believe he is saying such people are not Christians.

Christians and Their Sins

First John 2:1 deals with the sin issue for Christians. John emphatically says that we Christians have been given Biblical information so that we may not sin, but he consoles us by saying we have an Advocate, Jesus Christ the Righteous.

Some people believe to have an advocate in Jesus Christ means when we sin, he reminds the Father to not get too upset over it, because we are Christ's and our sins are forgiven due to his work on our behalf. In other words, God the Father has a bad memory, and thus he needs Jesus to constantly remind him which of us belong to him and which ones don't.

I think it is significant that his name here is not merely Jesus Christ, but Jesus Christ the Righteous. It

reminds us that we have a relationship with God the
Father based not on our performance, but rather on the
perfect righteousness of Jesus Christ. My sins no longer
mandate God's hostility toward me. Jesus Christ's
record is now my identity. This does not, of course,
mean that I may abuse this grace. Rather, as a recipient
of his perfectly sinless life, I am grateful beyond words.
His sinless life, also known as eternal Life, is now my
life, *When Christ who is our life appears, then you also
will appear with Him in glory* (Colossians 3:4). His life in
me resulted in new desires, a new identity and a
heightened world view. I can now state, without equiv-
ocation, that when a person becomes a Christian as
John advocates here, he is totally forgiven and he also
receives the advocate, Jesus Christ the Righteous, who
becomes his righteousness. Now he can have fellowship with other Christians, the Son, and the Father.

The Other Verses

Why do the verses in the gospels, such as those previ-
ously mentioned in Matthew 18, along with the Lord's
Prayer, place conditions on forgiveness? Simply
because Christ had not yet completed his work on our
behalf at the time he said these things. Jesus had not
yet died. He had not yet gained access for us to the
Father through His resurrection and enthronement, ...
[he has] raised us up together, and made us sit together

in the heavenly places in Christ Jesus (Ephesians 2:6).

In Matthew 18 believers had not yet become the righteousness of God, and sins were still being covered on a sacrifice-by-sacrifice basis. We know this by how the language changed in the epistles. We should not go back to the gospels to find our experience in these matters, just as we should not go back to the Jewish experience in the Old Testament to describe our current experience. Bill Gillham, in his book, *What God Wishes Christians Knew About Christianity* says, "Does the grace of God through Christ throw Christians to 'the torturers' until we forgive our brother from the heart? I refer you to God's Word for the answer: *Be kind to one another, tenderhearted, forgiving each other, just as God in Christ also has forgiven you* (Ephesians 4:32). We must primarily base our forgiveness doctrine on what God's Word says about our forgiveness after the cross."

We have the finished work of Christ available to us. It is my belief that if Christians try to obtain forgiveness after they have been forgiven, they are thereby minimizing that finished work. Let's not waste it by misunderstanding one verse—1 John 1:9. Let us, rather, be content to turn from our sins and obey the Lord out of gratitude, knowing our relationship with him is fixed forever in perfection.

Part 3

Results

.

Chapter Fifteen

We Would See Jesus

Many...can only distinguish between
good and evil; they cannot differentiate
life and death. The reason for this
is simply that they fail to see
that everything is in Christ.
Watchman Nee

There were problems in Jerusalem—big problems! There were always problems in Jerusalem, but these were different. Someone who had just come into town for the Passover might not have noticed them, but anyone who was familiar with the situation knew there were huge problems. People came to Jerusalem from all over for the Passover and they went to the temple and bought animals for their sacrifices. Their attention was centered on the chief priest and other leaders, but this year it was different. Something was wrong!

The people weren't asking about the Passover, and they weren't coming to the temple to buy the animals. Instead, they were exclaiming, "Where's Jesus? We want to see Jesus!"

This was a significant problem and put the leaders in a precarious position. The Romans had appointed them to be in charge of the Israeli nation, but things were rapidly deteriorating. People weren't following the norm. They were asking, "Where's Jesus?"

There were also rumors of a bigger problem. The Romans were concerned that the leaders might be losing control of the people. If the Romans took away the authority of the leadership, then they would lose their jobs. They had great grounds for concern.... *If we let Him alone like this, everyone will believe in Him, and the Romans will come and take away both our place and nation* (John 11:48).

At one point Caiaphas, the high priest, said it would be better if one man died than if the whole nation were to be lost. So they began to make plans to eliminate Jesus. They also planned to eliminate that troublesome friend of His, Lazarus. After all, if it weren't for Lazarus, the problems wouldn't have begun in the first place. The rumor was circulating that Jesus had raised this man from the dead after he had been in the grave for four days. People were coming from all over. They wanted to see Jesus, but they also wanted to see Lazarus. They were ignoring the chief priest and the rest of the leadership. They were supposed to be in town for the Passover, but that's not what they came for. They came to see Jesus!

The entire situation was quickly getting out of hand. Why couldn't people leave things as they had always been? Things had been fine, year after year after year. The Passover had been observed every year and there had always been good money to be made by selling the animals. Why did people always have to cause problems?

The Greeks

John records this during the Passover ....*there were certain Greeks among those who came up to worship at the feast. Then they came to Philip, who was from Bethsaida of Galilee, and asked him, saying, "Sir, we wish to see Jesus." Philip came and told Andrew, and in turn Andrew and Philip told Jesus. But Jesus answered them, saying, "The hour has come that the Son of Man should be glorified. Most assuredly, I say to you, unless a grain of wheat falls into the ground and dies, it remains alone; but if it dies, it produces much grain. He who loves his life will lose it, and he who hates his life in this world will keep it for eternal life. If anyone serves Me, let him follow Me; and where I am, there My servant will be also. If anyone serves Me, him My Father will honor.* (John 12:20-26).

"We want to see Jesus," was the cry of the crowds,

but the people were supposed to be coming for the Passover. The leadership was jealous and they were losing control of the crowds. Just a few days before, Jesus had come into town riding a donkey, with everybody yelling and screaming, "Hosanna, hosanna in the highest!" That was not what the Passover was supposed to be about! You'd think that at least these people coming all the way from Greece would be serious about their religion; but no—even they wanted to see this Jesus, the rabble-rouser.... *Nevertheless even among the rulers many believed in Him, but because of the Pharisees they did not confess Him, lest they should be put out of the synagogue; for they loved the praise of men more than the praise of God* (John 12:42-43).

Can you imagine Philip and Andrew having a little conversation, when the Greeks came saying, "We want to see Jesus?"

"Should we show them where Jesus is?"

"I don't know, we've heard rumors that people want to kill him."

"Maybe it's not our call; maybe we should let Jesus determine if he wants to see them."

"But what if Jesus doesn't give straight answers. You know he often doesn't give straight answers. Sometimes he starts talking about things they aren't even asking about. What if he does that?"

"I guess that's his privilege; he can say whatever he wants. He handles himself quite well, you know."

"All right, let's bring them to Jesus."

And Jesus says, *Unless a grain of wheat falls into the ground and dies, it remains by itself alone; but if it dies, it bears much fruit* (John 12:24).

Philip and Andrew's response might have been, "Say what? These Greeks want to see you; why are you talking about farming? What does that have to do with seeing you? Why cannot you just make yourself available? Why can't you give a straight answer? May they see you or not?"

The Grain of Wheat

John's quote of Jesus' statement raised a certain level of curiosity.

Have you ever wondered about his answer? What does that have to do with seeing Jesus? The Scriptures say Jesus knew he was about to be glorified. He knew his time on earth was coming to an end. The leaders wanted to eliminate him, and he realized that if people wanted to see him from that time forth, the one-on-one approach wasn't going to work.

If he died, how would the people see Jesus? He knew something else. He knew if he went away and came back, in Spirit, and filled those of us who trust him with his presence, then people everywhere could see Jesus. But Philip and Andrew didn't understand why Jesus spoke of seeds and neither did the Greeks.

What did Jesus Mean?

If you have ever lived on a farm, or if you have ever had gardens and flowerbeds, then you know what happens when you place seeds in the ground.

I grew up on a farm in Montana, where we seeded barley, winter wheat, and spring wheat. Every fall, my dad would plant about 1200 acres of grain. As that grain was placed in the ground, we would pray for rain. We knew that if we received rain to moisten the soil, in a few weeks those kernels of grain wouldn't look quite the same as they had when we put them in the ground. The outer shells of those kernels of grain had to be broken. They had to burst, they had to decay, they had to fall apart. Why?

In every kernel of grain there is life that has to come forth. We didn't dig up the kernel of grain, but if we had, we might have been concerned. In the ground the kernals become disfigured, bloated and broken. We might have thought our crops were dead and gone.

Fortunately, we knew that had to happen, in order that the life could come forth. We knew that if that life came forth, in the spring we could reap forty, sixty, eighty, a hundred fold from each kernel of grain.

Death Before Life

There's a principle here that Jesus was establishing, when He talked about the kernel of wheat that had to fall into the ground and die in order to bear fruit. If it didn't die it would always be one single, individual, solitary kernel of wheat, but if it died it would bring forth fruit. He was first of all talking about Himself, that He had to die in order to bear fruit, to multiply Himself throughout the world. But he was also talking about us, wasn't he? If you want to multiply the seed to bear fruit, it has to die. So the principle is this: if we want to bear fruit, if we want to see the life that God places inside of us—his life, Christ's life—manifested, then we have to go through whatever it takes for the outer shell, surrounding the life in us, to be broken.

This requires a deterioration, a falling apart. The Bible refers to it as suffering loss, or brokenness. If we're going to be broken so the life of Christ can come forth, we're also probably going to have to go through a humbling process. Why? Why does the process of humility precede the exaltation, as it did with Jesus, as it does with a kernel of wheat?

It's because of that outer shell. We know what the outer shell is in a kernel of wheat, but what does the outer shell represent in our lives? It represents our techniques, our manipulation, our control mechanisms, our coping skills, our religiosity. It represents all that we are, in and of ourselves, apart from Christ. The problem is that, even though the life of Christ came into us at the time we became Christians—at our new birth—we can still continue to live out of that outer shell. We have ways of making life work, especially if we grew up in the church.

Humility Before Exaltation

In the Scriptures, over and over again, we read the same passage many times and still miss the underlying principle. The Scriptures are replete with references to humility preceding glorification. In Philippians we read about Jesus' modeling of humility followed by glorification: *Who, although He existed in the form of God, did not regard equality with God a thing to be grasped, but empties Himself, taking the form of a bondservant. And being found in appearance as a man, He humbled Himself by becoming obedient to the point of death, even death on a Cross* (Philippians 2:5-8).

Often I've heard people say, "I could be under authority if I respected my authority, and I could be under authority if my authority loved me, treated me right." But did Jesus' authority treat Him right? What did His authority require of Him? Obedience, even unto death.

And what happened after Jesus died? Paul continues, *Therefore also God highly exalted Him, and bestowed on Him the name which is above every name, that at the name of Jesus every knee should bow,...and that every tongue should confess that Jesus Christ is Lord, to the glory of God the Father. So then, my beloved, just as you have always obeyed, not as in my presence only, but now (obey) much more in my absence...: for it is God who is at work in you, both to will and to work for His good pleasure* (Philippians 2:9-13). Jesus humbled Himself before he was glorified.

Other Scriptures express the same thing. In Proverbs we find many references to our need for humility. *The fear of the Lord is the instruction for wisdom, and before honor comes humility* (Proverbs 15:33). *Before destruction the heart of man is haughty, but humility goes before honor* (Proverbs 18:12). *The reward of humility and the fear of the Lord are riches, honor and life* (Proverbs 22:4).

Some of us may have been going through life never getting ahead, even though we've worked hard, we've tried hard. We've gone to school, we've done our best, we've put in our time, but we can't seem to get on top. Even our best, most intelligent decisions seem to get us nowhere. Have you thought about the possibility that humbling yourself and brokenness precede exaltation? Is there pride in your life?

The reward for humility and the fear of the Lord are riches and honor and life. We can do a lot in our self-sufficiency. We can make life work for awhile. We can even give all the glory to Christ and we can give all the honor to God for everything we accomplish out of our natural talents and abilities, but if it's self-exaltation, it's not God's exaltation. One Bible translation says that if we are living according to the flesh, we will die.... *For if you live according to the flesh you will die; but if by the Spirit you put to death the deeds of the body, you will live* (Romans 8:13). The word die, however, often refers to self-destruction or weakness carried to an ultimate measure. Or another translation renders that verse.... *So don't you see that we don't owe this old do-it-yourself life one red cent. There's nothing in it for us, nothing at all. The best thing to do is give it a decent burial and get on with your new life. God's Spirit beckons. There are things to do and places to go!* (Romans 8:13 MSG).

God's Exaltation vs. Self-Exaltation

How do you know if it's self-exaltation versus God's exaltation or self-sufficiency versus Christ's sufficiency? Christ's exaltation follows humility. Peter says it this way... *You younger men, likewise, be subject to your elders; and all of you, clothe yourselves with humility toward one another, for God is opposed to the proud, but gives grace to the humble. Humble yourselves therefore, under the mighty hand of God, that he may exalt you* (1 Peter 5:5-6). When? "....at the proper time." Self-exaltation, haughtiness, pride, self-glorification go hand-in-hand.

I'm a senior citizen now. I've been in a lot of churches and I often hear people talking about wanting to be used by God. I hear people saying, "Oh, I really need to witness for Christ." They just can't seem to get started. There's always a good reason why they're not multiplying. Is that true of you? Have you thought of the possibility that you're still just a single kernel of wheat because the life hasn't sprung forth? Has the life of Christ been able to spring forth, or have you been busy trying to make something out of yourself? Have you gone through the brokenness and the humbling that are necessary for life to spring forth? Do you want others to see Jesus in you? Brokenness and humility, a breaking of the outer shell, has to take place first.

We may not like it when that happens. Sometimes losing our life means suffering loss. Sometimes losing our life means going through things that we didn't have in mind as part of our self-exaltation. If you want to see Jesus in your life, it's absolutely necessary that you be willing to be like that kernel of wheat.

You may wonder why we have periodic economic slumps—people losing jobs, suffering economic loss, or losing their investments and retirement. It's painful! Do you know how many people are being humbled through these events? I'm not saying that all of these individuals are people whom God is breaking in the outer shell so inner life can come forth. However, you should be able to know if it's happening to you. You should know that if you've never been broken, it might be your time. There are all kinds of people who come to Christ for salvation, but they don't want anything to do with transformation. Transformation means that humility precedes exaltation.

It's not only economic failure that can break the outer shell. Fighting failure is exhausting! Are we willing to be the failure we are, so Christ can be everything he is in us? Maybe our whole support system has fallen away. Perhaps the people we love the most, have turned on us, and God is using our rejection to break the outer shell. All the self-sufficiency and self-reliance, everything that we thought was going to meet our needs, has suddenly disappeared. If that's what it takes so that you can see Jesus, are you willing?

We can fight so hard to hang onto everything important to us. Jesus said, if you really want to know life, you have to lose yours, lose that outer shell which you think is life. Perhaps you have gone through this already, so you know what that can mean. But if you haven't, let me describe three individuals who had to suffer loss in order that they might see Christ.

Three Examples

In his letter to the Philippians, Paul says that he had

everything going for him. He was the Jew of Jews. He was a Hebrew born of Hebrews. He was of the right tribe; he had been circumcised on exactly the eighth day and he said that when it came to zeal, he persecuted the church. When it came to righteousness under the law, he didn't make any mistakes.

The Bible says that Paul came to a point where he understood he could have no more confidence in the flesh. What does that mean? It simply means that I have no confidence in myself, in my self-sufficiency. We might say, "Paul, you need to see a therapist. It's not good to have such a poor self-esteem." But Paul knew what he was saying... *I count all things loss for the excellence of the knowledge of Christ Jesus my Lord, for whom I have suffered the loss of all things, and count them as rubbish, that I may gain Christ and be found in Him, not having my own righteousness, which is from the law, but that which is through faith in Christ, the righteousness which is from God by faith; that I may know Him and the power of His resurrection, and the fellowship of His sufferings, being conformed to His death* (Philippians 3:8-10).

What did it cost Paul to bear fruit? Everything! Everything he had worked for. All that he was, in and of himself. Everything he was by way of heritage. Do you want to see Jesus? It's going to cost everything.

Another example is a young man I worked with who had a great ministry, one that I admired probably more than any other, but his marriage was falling apart. He was bringing people to Christ, far more than anyone else I knew. He had established churches, but he was losing his marriage. I watched him saying all the right things, understanding the humbling necessary for exaltation, talking about exchanging his life, his self-life, for the Christ-life. He could talk to other people about it, but his own marriage was falling apart. When I talked with his wife, I found that in his relationship with her he was proud and arrogant, he thought he was a cut above others, including her. He didn't think she had the intelligence she needed to be his wife. Pride was coming out his ears! I wrote him the most scathing letter he ever received. I called him an arrogant, pompous so-and-so, and he received it. I felt I could be that honest because he was a friend.

God used that letter to break him of his self-sufficiency and his self-reliance. Everything in the outer shell was broken, so Christ could come forth. Today he's such a different man that his wife doesn't know how to act around him. She's never been loved by him this way before.

The final example is myself. I grew up in a Christian home, attended a Christian school and a Christian college. I went to church and was a church elder twice in my twenties. From the outside I looked good! But on the inside, I knew I was a mess. I was a therapist, but I couldn't conquer my own anxiety. I would try to help people overcome obstacles in their life, but I couldn't overcome the sin in my own life. I thought I had to maintain a facade, because everybody who knew me thought I was quite successful. I had a wonderful wife and four children, but I knew inside I was a failure at living the Christian life. I did my best to live for Jesus, but Jesus wasn't living through me. I knew nothing about brokenness. I didn't know that humility preceded exaltation.

My good friend Roger Alliman, who was a member of our Board of Directors for many years, has written numerous books. In his book, *Breaking The Self-Centered Life—Revised Edition*, he writes:

"In the process of spiritual maturity it is helpful for us as Christians to adjust our perspective to see that:

> • Painful experiences can be effective in bringing positive change to our lives.
> • The sins in our lives will be used by God to show us new things about his love, forgiveness, and grace.
> • Our Father is far more interested in doing something 'in' us than doing something 'for' us.

Pain, brokenness, testing, trials, suffering—they are all God's ways to use the world, the flesh, and the devil to stir his stubborn children into understanding that there is much more to life and purpose than merely this present age."

For me, at age 28, I was arrogant and proud—I had

the spiritual gift of criticism. I found fault with every-body and everything. I would get on my knees and say, "Oh Lord, I can't live the Christian life, but I'm going to try harder. And if you'll give me one more chance, I'll do my very best." But three things overwhelmed me: anxiety, inability to conquer sin, and not being able to find truth. I knew that in the New Testament people were transformed. Why didn't it happen to me when I came to Christ? Why was I such a mess?

God gradually began to show me that if I was to find peace over anxiety, it would have to be because he gave it to me. Although I had peace with God, I didn't have the peace that passes all understanding that kept my heart and mind by Christ Jesus... *and the peace of God, which surpasses all understanding, will guard your hearts and minds through Christ Jesus* (Philippians 4:7). I couldn't achieve peace on my own.

He began to show me that if I was to experience victory in my life, it would have to be because he was going to give me victory. I couldn't conquer sin, with or without his help. He began to show me if I was to find truth, it would have to be because he was going to reveal it to me—it wasn't coming from attending another conference or trying to find out why other people were more successful at helping others than I was. In reality, they weren't, but I was deceived into thinking they were. Truth such as I was seeking could not come by my mind alone.

I got on my knees and confessed to the Lord. I said, "Father, I am a total failure. I give up on myself. I have no more confidence in the flesh. I can't live the Christian life. I'm helpless. I'm hopeless. I ask you to do with me whatever you want to do." This prayer was prayed with great fear! I didn't trust God!

God was breaking my outer shell. Within days I came to the end of my own resources, in answer to the prayer. I humbled myself under the mighty hand of God.

It was a major turning point in my life. Two days later, Christ filled me with his presence in a way I'd never been filled before. The Scriptures came alive to me. I began to understand what it meant to experience his life for my life... *It is no longer I who live, but it is Christ who lives in me* (Galatians 2:20).

I experienced a total revolution that has continued to this day.

Do you want to see Jesus? You have a choice. You can remain a single, solitary kernel of wheat, sitting in a church pew week after week, not bearing fruit. Or, if you want the best that God has for you, if you want to experience his life, if you want to have a quality of life that will totally transcend the life of those living out of their own resources—then agree to be broken. Agree to fall into the ground and experience your death, so Christ may become pre-eminent in you and through you.

....unless a grain of wheat falls into the earth and dies, it can only be a single seed. But if it dies, it bears much fruit (John 12:24 CEB).

Acknowledgments

Roger Alliman was the encourager I needed to attempt this book. He has authored several books, was one of the founding officers of Rapha, and he organized and helped to create the syllabus and videos for our first conferences. Roger typed and corrected chapter by chapter. He is a jack of all trades and master of all. Thanks Roger for your confidence in me and obeying the Divine author in this endeavor. I admire your abiding life for helping me when you were going through your own fiery trial.

Dr. David Orison. I so value you as a brother in Christ. It is not easy to find a pastor-theologian commited to ultimate grace. You are that man that checked the correctness of my understanding of Scripture.

Candace LeFebre. I didn't know your many editing skills until embarking on this project. No wonder you were an A student and a superb wife for our son.

Betty, my wife. Thank you for your meticulous reading of this manuscript. You took the time to check and recheck spelling and many details which I missed and missed again.

Appendices

Kwiki Kwiz #1

1. T F I must try as a Christian to make my life more Christlike.
2. T F A Christian's chief goal in life is to sin less and less as he/she gets older.
3. T F I believe I will gradually grow closer to God as I mature as a Christian.
4. T F I am saved by the blood of the Lamb.
5. T F Conquering sin is something I don't have to do.
6. T F I am, thank the Lord, a forgiven sinner.
7. T F A Christian should ask for forgiveness repeatedly.
8. T F God will not give you more than you can bear.
9. T F God changed my identity in an instant when I became a Christian.
10. T F Freedom involves a lifelong struggle for a Christian.

Kwiki Kwiz #2

1. T F I must try as a Christian to make my life more Christlike.
2. T F A Christian's chief goal in life is to sin less and less as he/she gets older.
3. T F I believe I will gradually grow closer to God as I mature as a Christian.
4. T F I am saved by the blood of the Lamb.
5. T F Conquering sin is something I don't have to do.
6. T F I am, thank the Lord, a forgiven sinner.
7. T F A Christian should ask for forgiveness repeatedly.
8. T F God will not give you more than you can bear.
9. T F God changed my identity in an instant when I became a Christian.
10. T F Freedom involves a lifelong struggle for a Christian.

Appendix C

Unbeliever

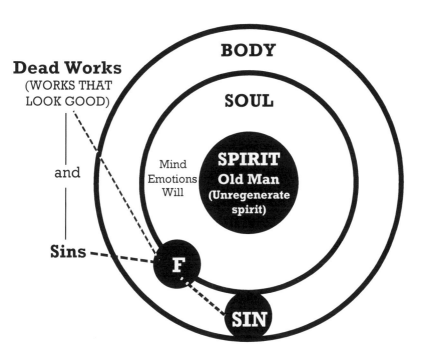

THE NON-CHRISTIAN

Temptation

Sin as a power from within and without

Attacks

Against the spiritually dead unbeliever
through the soul and body

He resists or succumbs

Flesh and law are his only resources
for resisting temptation

He responds

with either dead works or sins

Appendix D

Believer
See Graphic →

The believer has the option of yielding to two opposite sources. His spirit is now alive with the supernatural life of Christ, and he can yield himself to the Spirit via his will or he can yield himself to sin—the unholy force of temptation which is always with him. This freedom is not available to the unbeliever. If the believer yields to sin, he will commence operating according to the flesh—usually temporarily—but if he yields himself to the Spirit, he will be living according to the Spirit. Thus the believer has a supernatural life, and is permanently in a supernatural position in the heavenly places at the right hand of God. Thus he should always deal with temptation from a position of having conquered it, because he was in Christ when Christ conquered it. His relationship with the devil's wiles are no different than Christ's relationship with the devil's wiles. We are in union with Christ!

Appendix D

Believer

Seated with Christ in the heavenlies Eph 2:6

BODY

GoodWorks

SOUL

OR

SPIRIT
New Man
(C)
(Regenerate spirit)

Mind
Emotions
Will

Sins · · · F

SIN

OLD † MAN

Romans 6:6a
Ezekiel 36:25-27

Appendix E

Terminology

Other Translations	King James Version
Old Man	
Old Self	Old Man
Old Nature	
Self or Self-Life	
Flesh	Flesh
Sinful Nature	
Sin (Power of Sin)	Sin

Appendix F

Carnality

The terminology used in Romans 8 is wonderfully precise if we use a Bible that is accurately translated. We too need to be precise in how we use the language of God. The following diagram can help us understand the adjectives God used.

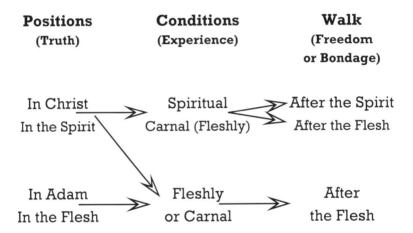

Positions	**Conditions**	**Walk**
(Truth)	(Experience)	(Freedom or Bondage)

In Christ
In the Spirit → Spiritual → After the Spirit
Carnal (Fleshly) → After the Flesh

In Adam
In the Flesh → Fleshly or Carnal → After the Flesh

Some versions substitute "according to the Spirit" for "after the Spirit." Thus, a Christian can never be in the flesh, but he can walk after the flesh. Then he is carnal, or fleshly. A non-Christian is always in the flesh, but never in the Spirit. He is fleshly, or carnal, and can only walk after the flesh. See the following verses: Romans 8:5, 6, 8, 9, 12, 13.

Bibliography

Alliman, Roger. *Breaking the Self-Centered Life — Revised Edition* Colorado Springs, 2003. www.alliman.com

Ewing, Bill. *Rest Assured.* Real Life Press, Rapid City, SD. 2003

Edwards, Gene. *Exquisite Agony.* The Seed Sowers, Jacksonville, FL. MCMXCIV

Gillam, Bill. *Lifetime Guarantee.* Wolgemuth & Hyatt, Brentwood, TN 1987

Gillam, Bill. *What God Wishes Every Christian Knew About Christianity,* Harvest House Publishing, Eugine, OR, 1998

Hunt, June. *Seeing Yourself Through God's Eyes.* Dallas, TX 2004. www.hopefortheheart.org

Nee, Watchman. *The Normal Christian Life.* Christian Literature Crusade, Montreal, Canada 1961

Smith, Greg and Stone, Dan. *The Rest of the Gospel.* One Press, Richardson, TX 2000

Solomon, Charles R. *Handbook to Happiness.* Tyndale, Carol Stream, IL 1971, 1989, 1999

●　●　●

Additional insight into the topics covered in this book
are also available on a DVD or CD series by
Lee LeFebre
The Grace Life Conference
along with a corresponding syllabus
from
www.thelifebookstore.com
720-248-7211

Notes

Notes